THE PEOPLE BUSINESS

The Story of Selling as It Affects Our Lives

David Namer

LifeRich Publishing is a registered trademark of The Reader's Digest Association, Inc.

LifeRich Publishing books may be ordered through booksellers or by contacting:

LifeRich Publishing
1663 Liberty Drive
Bloomington, IN 47403
www.liferichpublishing.com
1 (888) 238-8637

ISBN: 978-1-4897-1634-7 (sc)
ISBN: 978-1-4897-1635-4 (hc)
ISBN: 978-1-4897-1633-0 (e)

Library of Congress Control Number: 2018938684

Print information available on the last page.

LifeRich Publishing rev. date: 04/20/2018

Contents

Dedicated to Alexandra Vivian Namer

Part I

Foreword

The Case for The People Business

Forged by the experiences of life, trained by the best minds that ever traveled this earth, inspired by the indomitable courage and persistence of will of my daughter, Alexandra, and desirous of improving human relationships, I wrote this book to help each person who reads it to better their lives by communicating more effectively.

Simply stated, communicating is the imparting of something to someone else. Communication is the essence of sales. For sales is nothing short of communicating to people something they are lacking, which they need, and which can be identified: an idea, product, fact, or feeling. So to be successful at life, we need to learn to sell.

Therefore, if we want to be successful at life, we need to learn how to sell, which means we need to learn how to communicate. If we do not communicate clearly, we risk being misunderstood, and that leads to strife, discord, and unhappiness.

I dedicate my book to every man, woman, and child who wants to succeed in life. I know that anyone who reads this book will find something in it that will change their life for the good. I dedicate my book to my daughter, Alexandra "Lexi" Vivian Namer, who has taught me to never give up, to never be discouraged, and to never lose belief in myself.

Every person who lives, walks, and breathes should understand that the basic principles upon which the fabric of their lives are woven derive from salesmanship; (i.e., communications). Regardless of who we are or what we do, regardless of what walk of life we are in, we are all involved in selling, whether ourselves, a product, our ideas, a service, or a relationship.

A boy meets a girl and, through the process of selling, convinces her that he is the one for her; he sells her on how great he is, or how good he will be for her, listing all the reasons why she should go out with him. This is selling. He is selling himself. And this is just one example of how the principles of selling apply to our daily lives.

Physicians who are involved in a specialty field depend on their selling ability to attract patients. They depend on general practitioners to refer business to them. Now, these general practitioners won't send business to doctors who don't share their beliefs or the desire to place the interests of their patients first. They won't refer patients to a specialist who is going to leave a bad taste in their mouth.

It is important for everyone, in every walk of life, to understand and master the principles that are at work in selling. Not only are we selling; we are also being sold. We have all felt and experienced these principles used against us. Sales is a dynamic process; it involves two-way communication. Whenever two people are involved in business, a conveyance of ideas, or an exchange of feelings, selling is taking place. Each person is either selling or being sold. Understanding the principles involved in this dynamic will make us more aware of the process and better prepare ourselves for when they are used against us. That will turn those experiences into more productive and rewarding times.

The People Business puts the sales profession on a very high plane. It makes the case that salesmanship is practiced to some degree by everyone. Everyone is involved in the people business, all of us. From the first days of Adam and Eve, we have been trying to sell others on our own ideas, beliefs, viewpoints, or services. Eve was the first salesperson when she sold Adam on the idea of eating the apple. And what a salesperson she was. Here was

Adam, all the comforts of paradise and no worries, and yet Eve convinced him that he would have a better life if he ate the apple.

You may think that man could recognize on his own what is beneficial and what is necessary for his betterment or for his existence, but he really can't. Man is resistant to change and will fight change all the way down the line. Man is ignorant of change; he does not always recognize the beneficial value of it. We must be sold; sold on an idea, sold on a product, sold on a service. This is why salespeople are so important in society today and have been since the beginning of time. And they will probably continue to be, no matter how far we progress.

This is why the artist and the writer, who are both innovators, are attacked by society. It is not that the consumer is too dumb to know what is good for him. It is not that man is dumb in the sense of not being educated or not knowing what's going on around them. It's simply that we are ignorant about the new things going on, unaware of the changes being made.

The fundamental aspects of persuasion are suggestion and logical reasoning, suggestion taking precedence and probably more important than logical reasoning. Human beings are not essentially reasoning creatures. In fact, most people scarcely reason at all. All of their actions are usually the result of imitation, habit, or suggestion. Most of their actions, and psychologists will bear this out, are only reactions. The average person accepts as true every idea or conclusion that enters his mind, unless a contradictory idea blocks this acceptance.

Additionally, the average person will act according to an idea or action that enters his mind unless he is blocked by a physical obstacle or a contrary idea. This is the principle upon which the foundation of most of our modern- day advertising is based, the fact that statements that are repeated and not denied will tend to be accepted.

The salesperson uses those principles during the presentation and close. He will often fill out the order, thereby suggesting an act of writing. When he hands the prospect a pen with the suggestion, "Please okay this agreement where indicated," the prospect will generally go along with the idea.

A Peace Corps worker in South America trying to teach Indians to drink only water that has been boiled would be just as interested to pick up this book, as would be a less scrupulous type who wishes to utilize persuasion to sell something that was not needed.

When I sat down to write this book, I reflected on my many years in sales; I really like sales. It should be noted that I have sold everything from vacuum cleaners to encyclopedias to magazines to coffee, door-to-door; I've also provided financial services. I have sold commodities, including flour, rice, wheat, cement, lemon oil, and even olive oil to Italy. During this time, my mind was constantly thinking of ways to improve the occupation, to upgrade sales and make it more professional. I wanted to bring salesmanship out of the drummer image and spread that professionalism to all salespeople, regardless of what they are selling.

That is why I entitled the book *The People Business*. The Peace Corps worker would be just as apt to pick it up as would someone selling vacuum cleaners. It is applicable in all phases of life. I feel that I've compiled something that can be used by everyone. My contention is that everyone is selling in their day-to-day interactions with other people. I am selling my ideas to you. Whether I get my ideas across to you or not determines the success of my presentation, regardless of whether there is a sale or not.

Many people have the wrong impression of salespeople, either through naiveté or bad experiences, actual or perceived. The best example of this is the insurance industry. There was a time when people had a negative image of an insurance salesman: the sloppy, shirt-sleeved person driving through rural sections, banging on doors to get people to buy insurance through high pressure, threatening people, using out-and-out coercion, threatening loss of life, limb, or property. The last thing people wanted to see was an insurance salesman. Therefore, the insurance industry spent great sums of money promoting the image of the neat, trained professional counselor.

Salesmanship is not inherent. There are born salespeople, though very few of them. To be efficient and successful, one must be trained in sales.

This training must include more than attending a seminar and listening to people who are successful speak about their achievements.

Selling is individualistic; you may hear how someone made a sale, but that particular strategy may not apply to you. What works for you may not work for me. But the general concepts of selling are universal; they must be formulated, nurtured, and grasped. Only then will a particular strategy fall into place, just like a puzzle.

The importance of knowing your product cannot be overemphasized. You must have all the answers for anticipated questions. And you can only gain this knowledge if you are willing to listen a lot. It's fine to talk, but if you don't get a dialogue going, it's almost impossible to get an indication of your progress, feedback, as it were.

Honesty and straightforwardness is indispensable to succeeding in any endeavor. My career has been dedicated to honesty and legitimacy. The question is how, or where, to draw the line as to what is good and evil, black and white. The presentation must be effective, yet it must involve the principles to be set forth herein. It is okay to approach the line, as long as you do not go over it. I advocate a judicious approach. The line sometimes gets blurry; sometimes, you cannot draw a line. Each case must be approached individually.

The product you are selling, and the needs of those to whom you are selling, will dictate how your presentation will be formed. For example, suppose I was selling quality encyclopedias to a family who could afford it. Assume that their children need and want the set. In this case, I could apply more pressure than normal. I wouldn't take the approach that the children would grow up ignorant, that they would fail in society, that they won't complete high school or get into college. What I would say is that the children would not have the advantages of their peers. In the schools today, given the overcrowded classrooms, teachers do not have time for individual instruction. They tend to give class projects. They say, "Go home and look this up in your reference set," assuming that all families have reference sets. Now sure, you can look that up in the public library, if one is available. But can you see forty people descending upon a single reference volume all at once?

What usually happens is that after five or six people, someone gets tired of waiting around the library and rips out the page to bring home. What does your child do then? I deliberately referred to a reference set as opposed to my own set because I didn't want to imply that without *my* set, the kids will grow up ignorant. It's a case of semantics. You are doing something that you believe is beneficial for that family. You know that sooner or later, someone is going to sell them a set of encyclopedias.

Equally important, another salesperson could be selling an inferior product, so I feel that it would be to their advantage to get something of quality, something that the family can make good use of.

Another example of this issue, the moral dilemma facing salespeople, deals with selling quality products in less-than-affluent areas. A poor woman may purchase a shoddy knife for a dollar. Two weeks later, that knife will break; she'll have to purchase another, and so on. Over a period of time, she will have invested more money in knives than the ten dollars she could have if she had bought a quality knife to begin with. This would have benefitted her in the long run.

The same issue occurs with salespeople who convince someone to buy a quality insurance product. Perhaps after the sale, your customer becomes dissatisfied with the premium and gives you a lot of grief. How can this be handled? You have to consider yourself in a positive light. You must believe in the beneficial aspects of your product. Sure, the premiums are a bit of a drag now, but looking into the future, the customer will soon have something of value, probably more than he would have had if he had tried saving alone. If you do something deceitful, it is difficult to visualize yourself as beneficial. If you view yourself as beneficial, it is easy to live with criticism.

It is important to delineate between a warm prospect that comes to you after realizing he needs your product or service and a cold one you approach, someone who is completely in the dark as to who you are and what you are selling.

The guy who approaches you has a need, a problem, and is seeking help. This is problem solving. The cold prospect doesn't know that he needs your product or service. A mental trauma takes place in the cold prospect; chances are that he went all through his life without knowing or caring that he needed your product or service. The moment you approach him, you have thrown cold water on him. The way in which you arouse his awareness has a profound effect upon the outcome of your presentation. This is why the psychology of selling is so important as emphasized herein.

On another track, there are times when a salesperson has built up the customer to the point of purchase; to what extent is the customer begging the salesperson to help make the purchase decision?

Life is a game that becomes competitive only when everyone is playing by the same rules or, at least, is aware of the rules. The rules must be clearly stated to all contestants. You must be sure that all contestants play by the same set of rules. This is one of the major points of *The People Business*. This is way I have subtitled it *The Story Selling as It Affects Our Lives*.

This might be a quirk of my thinking, but it's all right to take advantage of someone to whom you've explained the rules, by using the rules or the fine print, as long as you have made everyone aware that the fine print exists and that others have the equal opportunity of using that rule against you.

Take a company purchasing agent and a salesman. When a contract is written, it should clearly state the terms under which the product is delivered and under what conditions. Generally, there exists a penalty clause. The purchasing agent specifies a delivery date, and the seller accepts, knowing that he cannot deliver on time, but he needs that contract. The buyer has covered himself, knowing that the penalty clause will cover his company and insure speedy delivery. Each has taken advantage of the other.

To be sure, it is not the duty or place of a salesman to teach the customer a lesson. The sole function of the salesman is to sell his product, period. He may, by his function as product advocate, teach the customer a lesson, but any subsequent bad publicity may be detrimental to him and his product.

The salesman must pay heed to public relations. He must maintain a professional approach.

The buyer has no obligation to the salesman. The obligations of the sale rest solely on the shoulders of the salesman. It is incumbent upon the salesman to insure that he remains professional at all times and to insure that he follows the tenets specified herein, including qualification of your prospect. The salesman is the professional. It is his business to distinguish what constitutes a legitimate buyer from an unqualified buyer. If he cannot, he needs to be retrained and needs to read this book even more. My book covers the fact that salespeople must know their product and every step in the production of that product. They also need to know about their competitors so as to judge their own product. Many firms consider salespeople to be their intelligence-gathering force. It's the duty of the salesperson to scout out his competition.

When you go into a firm, the first person you usually meet is a secretary or receptionist. You must woo this girl to get her on your side. She helps you with your sale by making the buyer more accessible. You are selling yourself, and that is a very good quality. That is why there is a section in the book explaining how to handle receptionists and secretaries. This falls neatly into the category of intelligence gathering.

Salespeople must be astute listeners. They must sense which way the customer is leaning. Second, they must give customers greater confidence to make up their own mind. And in order to do this, they must be able to adapt to the customer's needs. Adaptability is a trait that all salespeople must possess. They must always be ready to confront new selling situations and cope with them. They must realize that they cannot change people. Rather, people change only when they want, and it is the salesperson's role to motivate that person to want to make that change. They must always be positive in their mental outlook.

The basic principle on which the world of selling is founded is confidence or trust. Therefore, it is the salesperson's job not only to exude these qualities, but also to create a trusting relationship with his customer.

Another aspect of self-confidence is pride and the desire to feel important. All of us want to be appreciated and to be complimented. People must feel they are of some importance, and they crave recognition from others.

The sole function of a salesperson is to make a sale, within the ethics and morality of sound business practices. Everything he does to make that sale falls within the parameters of being professional. A customer who comes in and wants to spend his money should be able to, and if the salesperson can coax him to spend more than intended, that's fine. Usually, if the salesperson can convince the customer to buy, that is sufficient proof that the customer wants the product.

And lastly, the only certainty of success is to be mentally and physically prepared to do your job. You may ask, "What if I am not mentally ready or not all fired up to make a presentation or perform my job functions, what is lost? Is someone who is working hard to present a case bringing value by advocating in a high-pressure effort, as opposed to a low-pressure, just trying to get by? Is this selling?"

The answer is a resounding yes! You are selling yourself or your ideas. What is being interjected into the situation is a touch of realism, humanity, and warmth. You are getting away from the mechanistic process wherein you merely do A, B, C, and so on; choose any one, all, or none. Just because the facts are stated in black and white does not mean there is not a human element in there somewhere. And this human element is sales.

Part II

Preface

Having been involved in sales for the better part of my life, I have learned that there are very few born salespeople. My experience has shown that 90 percent of the salespeople in the world today are trained. All of my life, I have been involved in selling various products, ideas, services, and programs, as well as formulating training programs for various businesses.

Realizing that the sales industry is one of the most lucrative professions today, my company, The People Business-Inc, set out to devise and implement a sales training and motivation course to produce trained professional salespeople capable of competing successfully. And though this course was intended primarily for salespeople, my background in public relations and advertising led me to conclude that it could also be used by anyone to further their own abilities and chances for success in other endeavors.

As Irving Allen so aptly put it, "The degrees of success we meet with in making other people want what we have to offer absolutely and positively govern the return we gain from life. And making other people want what we have is predicated on our ability to sell as much as on that which we are selling."

However, after scouring the libraries for any relevant material on selling, after consulting with different organizations already involved in sales training, and after attending many seminars and discussions concerning sales training, I discovered that there was not one single source that embodied all the various aspects of sales and sales training. In order to develop a comprehensive scope of the subject, it was necessary to absorb bits and pieces from many different sources.

Today's world is moving at an exceptionally rapid rate; time is of the essence. And, understanding the public's demand for efficiency and expediency, we organized our training manual to be a single source of complete sales information to the reading public.

Drawing on the experiences and ideas of some of the leading salespeople and trainers, we have encompassed all of the aspects of salesmanship under one cover. As you read through the following pages, as the story of selling unfolds for you, beginning with the importance of selling and concluding with ideas for self-instruction and motivation, it will become obvious why we have such a sense of accomplishment in this endeavor.

It is true that the basic aspects of selling remain constant, regardless of geographic area or the type of sales. It is to these basic concepts that we address ourselves in this book, feeling that much more is required in training sales personnel than merely having them listen to successful salespeople talk about their success. Rather, we should train, instruct, and teach those explicit ways in which one can become a successful, accomplished salesperson.

Rather than just have students attend seminars in which they are motivated for the moment, we should stress, describe, and explain the theory behind motivation and ways in which they can motivate themselves and maintain a positive mental attitude.

This, then, is our ultimate goal. And we feel that if readers of this book practice what they learn, they cannot help but become a success not only in sales but also in life, as well.

Part III

What Is a Salesperson?

Sitting at his desk, hunched over, with the only light on in the entire building illuminating his desk, the little man was feverishly adding the finishing touches to a report he was working on.

As he sat there working, the phone rang; he answered the phone, and the voice from the other end said, "Hello, Sam. Is the report on Amalgamated Oil complete?"

"Yes, Mr. Stevens," Sam answered. "I'm adding the finishing touches now."

"Remember, Sam, I need it on my desk by 9: 30 tomorrow morning."

"I remember, Mr. Stevens," Sam replied. "Don't worry. It will be finished in time."

With the conversation concluded, there was silence in the room once again as Sam returned to his work.

The next morning, Mr. Stevens entered his sprawling office at 9:25. As he walked past the receptionist, we can see the office, which was concealed in the dark; it is very plush, and at the rear is a door with a placard reading "Bryan M. Stevens Consultants, Inc." Mr. Stevens proceeded past his private secretary into his office, and as he did so, the intercom announced that Mr. Jenton and Mr. Pierce from Amalgamated Oil were waiting to see him. He glanced over his desk until he spotted the voluminous report with the name "Amalgamated Oil" on the cover. He then said, "Send them in."

As Pierce and Jenton entered the office, Mr. Stevens said, "Gentlemen, please be seated while I glance through this report for a final check."

Mr. Stevens looked through the report and signed his name to the last page as he nodded his approval. He then handed the report to the two men. They looked through it and commended Mr. Stevens for his usual very good work. They handed Mr. Stevens a check for $50,000, thanked him, and walked out, looking happy.

After they left, Mr. Stevens called in his secretary and asked, "Jan, how much am I paying Sam?"

"Two hundred dollars per week" was the reply.

"Give him a raise to $250," he replied.

In this very brief story, we have captured the essence of selling and salesmanship. Before Mr. Stevens hired him, Sam was doing odd jobs and working as a consultant on the side for only $125 per week. Although educated and gifted, with a very sharp mind, he did not have the ability to market and sell himself.

Mr. Stevens, on the other hand, was very smooth and confidence inspiring, but he only lasted a short time in each job. You see, Mr. Stevens was short on talent, but he was a very good salesman. He could sell himself and could accrue confidence in himself; at this he was very successful, and as long as he had people like Sam to do the work for him, he would continue to do well. And although Sam had great potential, he lacked the ability to sell himself and thus was content to work for Mr. Stevens, as he was now making more money than ever before.

This brings us to the point of why selling is important. Salesmanship plays a prime role in the exchange of goods and services. The function of a salesperson is to bring about a mutually advantageous exchange of goods or services. Success is fundamentally a matter of salesmanship and using its principles properly and effectively. The application of these principles may vary, but the basic principles remain the same. Everyone has something to sell, regardless of who or what or where you are.

By definition, a sale is the act of giving something up in return for something else. The "buyer" (obtainer) then, as we will use the term, is the one "returning something of value" for that which the "seller" (presenter) is "giving up". In this dynamic, both the buyer and seller have to ascribe relative value to that which is in play. The degree to which the seller and buyer are brought to agree that the value is equal will determine the result of the encounter. Thus, selling can also be considered the act of reaching/establishing equilibrium. We will develop both of these ideas as we proceed.

And, I would be remiss if I did not point out that the "commission" that salespeople earn is nothing more than the reward that he seeks, whatever form that takes, for his efforts.

Sales is more than just a matter of influencing another by argument or reason or conversation to purchase some concrete article or service or idea.

Everyone, all of us, is involved in the people business. But what is the people business? It is nothing less than the day-to-day contact and involvement of people, which I call selling.

From the days of Adam and Eve, people have been trying to sell others their ideas, beliefs, viewpoints, or services. Eve was the first salesperson when she sold Adam on the idea of eating the apple. And what a salesperson she was. Here was Adam, all the comforts of paradise and no worries, and yet Eve convinced him that he could have a better life if he ate the apple.

That started the world. Even then, with only two people in the world, it took sales to start the ball rolling. And the ball has continued to roll ever since, as the result of the salesperson.

In general, people don't always know what they want or what's best for them. We are static creatures, seeking equilibrium; we fear progress and react negatively to new ideas, discoveries, or innovations.

It is a salesperson's job to convince people that these ideas or discoveries, services or products, are for the betterment and enrichment of their lives. It is the role of salespeople to push these ideas or products to every corner of the globe. For by so doing, there is set up a constant line of communication, allowing exchanges of ideas and knowledge.

Sales is the essence upon which we have built our civilization; without it, our society would decay into a mass of isolated subunits, each with no connection to the other. Selling is nothing less than communications! For it is through selling that the exchange of ideas flows freely. And this exchange of ideas and services has hastened our emergence from the caves into this sprawling, complex society of ours.

But what is a salesperson? More specifically, who is a salesperson? The answer is very simple but often lost in the fast pace of today's life. Everyone is a salesperson. Every person who lives and breathes and is not isolated is a salesperson and has something to sell.

From the little boy who convinces his parents that he is old enough to stay by himself without a sitter to the salesman who just wrote an order for a million dollars, everyone is involved in selling. The little boy is trying to sell his parents on the idea that they should have confidence in him; his method for doing so revolves around his past behavior, his present abilities, and the advantages of not having to get a sitter. The boy points out that he has been very good in the past and that his parents had very good control over him. He appeals to the parents' pride by showing how much he has learned from them and how much they can depend on him. He concludes his "presentation" by pointing out that they no longer have to find a reliable sitter or worry about the expense involved.

The salesperson uses a very similar approach. He must build up confidence in himself. He does so by demonstrating an understanding of the needs and business of his prospects. He then proceeds to show why his product is best and concludes by pointing out the advantages of his prospect having that product. At the conclusion of his presentation, he takes the order.

Why Is Selling Important?

To quote Red Moatly, "Nothing happens until somebody sells something." And this is the fundamental key to life. To take the definition of sales in its purest essence, it is defined as the transfer of goods and services from seller to buyer, with benefit to the buyer and at a profit to the seller.

Now imagine for a moment, if you will, the owner of a factory that is producing at an unbelievable rate (which is what's taking place today) and yet lacking the sales force to sell his goods; he ends up with a stockpile of goods, with no place to store it.

Now, he may have the finest, highest quality product on the market, yet for the lack of the single most important ingredient in our economy, the sales staff, he goes bankrupt and loses his business.

Salespeople keep the wheels of our economy turning. And as Andrew Carnegie said, "You can take away my factories and my money, but leave my salesmen, and I will be back to where I am in less than two years. For all the millions of dollars of equipment and products to sell would do me absolutely no good had I not had any salesmen with which to sell my products."

The ability to handle people is probably the basic principle underlying leadership in any field of endeavor. People holding responsible positions in government, labor organizations, teachers, and heads of research organizations, as well as lawyers, doctors, and businesspeople, are confronted daily with the necessity of getting along with others. And here's the main point: The ability to handle people is nothing less than salesmanship under another name.

Leaders are leaders because they have followers. Their main task then as leaders is to persuade their followers to do what they want them to do. If they are unable to motivate these people, if they are unable to sell their followers on doing what they want them to do, then they cease to be leaders. Many expert physicians, architects, engineers, scientists, and lawyers are unable to advance professionally simply because they do not recognize the presence of a selling problem in their work.

People who apply the principles and fundamental attributes of salesmanship in their daily relationship with others, and develop the art of getting along with their neighbors and colleagues, will have friends and will be popular. Everyone, at one time or another, longs for friendship and popularity. We want to be accepted in life. Salespeople are accepted because they have studied the problem and know that they can sell more if they are well liked. And as sort of a footnote, the fact that they are accepted and liked is an end in itself. It increases their happiness as well as those they come in contact with.

The functions of salespeople in today's society are various, yet despite the demands placed on them by the changing times, there are several main concerns they must always address. Salespeople must dispense innovations and must possess knowledge. They must facilitate the consumption of products, act as a channel of communication for the market, and service their trade. Without a salesperson, the process of introducing innovation would be greatly impeded because people have neither the time nor the desire to seek out the newest developments in their field.

These people cannot possibly keep informed as to all the innovations affecting their particular field of interest.

This brings to mind a very common, although trite, expression used by many. I believe it was Emerson who first coined this expression, and I also believe he was a little removed from the realities of life as it exists today when he said that "if you build a better mousetrap the world will beat a path to your door". He forgot that without a salesperson, the world would not know of your latest mousetrap, much less would they know the location of the door.

Innovations, regardless of their merits or how earthshattering they may be, do not sell themselves. Eli Whitney could find no buyers for his cotton gin and was so impoverished at one point in his life that he had to borrow a suit of clothes to make a public speech.

Joseph Jacquard, the French inventor of the loom that promised to revolutionize the production of lace, was beaten and mobbed by fellow townspeople because they thought that he was robbing them of their opportunity to earn a living.

Charles Newbold invented an iron plow in 1797. He expected that the plow would quickly take the place of the clumsy and short-lived wooden plows that were then in use. The wooden plows would only scratch the surface of the soil, and they were so dull that it required several oxen to pull one, whereas the new iron plow not only penetrated the ground more deeply, it could be pulled by one team of oxen. However, Newbold struggled for many years to convince farmers that the iron plow would not poison the soil and that they would not kill the seeds planted in it.

It took King Gillette 5 years to finally sell his first seven safety razors.

Without aggressive selling, our economy would bog down, and new and improved products and services could not be brought forward for the betterment of our lives. Thomas Edison had to light an entire office building for free before anyone would even look at his electric light.

Elias Howe's sewing machine was smashed by a Boston mob.

When the idea of a railroad was first announced, it was scoffed at by the people. There were all sorts of jokes and wives' tales that traveling that fast would stop the circulation of the blood. George Westinghouse was ridiculed and called a fool because he claimed that he could stop a train with wind. Imagine that, stopping a train, which no one wanted or believed in in the first place, by wind.

I suppose that it's ironic that Samuel Morse had to plead with Congress many times before they would just look into (not even accept) his idea of the telegraph.

These are examples that the public doesn't go around demanding things. They have to be sold. People have to be taught what they want. They have to be shown that new inventions, new ideas, and new products are better for them. In other words, they have to be sold.

Problem solving is the changing of passiveness into action. He who can solve problems is the most desirable person in the world. Riches are his, along with everlasting friendship and popularity. This is the quintessential function of the salesman. The salesman approaches every situation from the perspective of what do I want and how do I get it.

This perspective permeates everything that the salesman does and how he does it. Equally important, approaching every person from the standpoint that they have a problem that needs resolution allows them to discover the motivation, the persuasion, used to create the acceptance of what the salesman is proposing.

First things first: what is a problem? A problem is any doubtful or difficult situation or experience that requires a solution. In other words, for our purposes, a problem is anything that acts as a barrier to the achievement of our goals, which can be anything that you desire, want, need, or perceive.

Identifying a problem is, essentially, setting goals. Defining the problem requires that we perceive and understand the barriers to achievement of those goals. If there are no barriers, then there is no problem. A problem only exists when there are barriers to achieving goals. Thus, the first step is the identification or establishment of our goals and the barriers to achieving them.

The ability to clearly articulate the problem (goals) leads to the ability to define the barriers to our achievement of our goals. Obvious? Yes! But equally obvious is how critical and overlooked this is. For, more often than not, little, if no, consideration is given to our goals, much less how to achieve them.

It cannot be overstated how important it is to overcome these barriers, these objections, to our goal. This is what we mean by "closing the sale". "Closing the sale" *is* the achievement of our goals, our objectives, and/or our dreams.

The solutions that we apply have to be manifested in a clear and decisive manner. Now is when we have to bring our training, which has been ingrained and reinforced through practice and repetition, into play.

The more information we can obtain, the clearer the definition will be. And, how do we get information? We ask, or are asked, questions. So, questions are an essential part of the communication/sales process. Understanding this greatly increases our effectiveness.

But let's also bear in mind that even well-established products still require selling. Millions of new buyers enter the market each year, buyers who have not heard the salesperson's story. Every product is new and unfamiliar to many potential buyers, and even the old familiar products are constantly being improved, and each improvement must be sold.

Although there are many different ideas, products, and services being advanced by salespeople, the objective of this book is to reach a comprehensive level of knowledge in the field of selling, to reach a level in the field of sales that everybody, regardless of their walk of life, will be able to use the principles and outlines contained herein for a successful and enriched life.

This book cannot introduce the various types of sales that occur and delineate their respective positions or their historical functions. I maintain that regardless of what you do, who you are, or what your level of achievement has been, after reading the contents of this book, and after a thorough understanding of this manual, you will take a giant step forward in terms of enriching your life and helping yourself on the road to success.

Sales is applicable in everyday life, in everyday living, and this is the universal trend that I want to convey. Whenever we are engaged in interpersonal relationships, whether we are communicating an idea, trying to convey our feelings or emotions, trying to sell a product, or trying to convince someone to do something, the dynamics at play are exactly the same.

There are many examples to prove that every situation in which two or more people are participating involves selling, whether themselves, their ideas, or their abilities. Even a player on the football team is trying to convince his coach that he is the best for that position. He does this by demonstrating his ability, dedication, and willingness to achieve his full potential. But further, after he has made the sale, he must then be capable of performing up to his stated capacity, or the sale will be rescinded (he'll wind up back on the bench).

The child who uses deceit and trickery to convince his parents to let him stay by himself; the salesman who uses distortion of the truth and high pressure in order to make a sale; or the football player who fails to live up to his stated ability or potential may have a short-sighted, temporary sale. But their credibility and sincerity have been damaged beyond repair. And more probable than not, the sale each of them made is likely to be rescinded (or be the last sale that will be made by that person).

The Sales Profession

The basic principle on which the world of selling is founded is confidence or trust. Salespeople must build confidence in themselves before they can make a sale. And the precepts behind building confidence and trust are the same, irrespective of who employs them or for what purpose. And these fundamental principles of salesmanship may be used two ways: directly, through words, the tone of voice, the actual words, and the truthfulness of same, and indirectly, through how we behave, how we comport ourselves, and the appearance we convey.

In other words, in order to effectively sell, you must be professional. And this applies to your everyday life as well; in order to accrue confidence and self-respect, you must comport yourself in a manner that will elicit these responses from others. In the game of life, which we all play, the ability to sell yourself or your ideas dictates the eventual winners in terms of success.

In order for sales to be ranked as a profession, salespeople must master several practical skills and display a special knowledge. And this knowledge should be obtainable through a recognized educational process, either through a college, university, or other professional or trade school.

In order for a salesperson to achieve professional standing, the special fund of knowledge and skill in dealing with practical affairs must be employed in such a way that the exchange of goods, services, and ideas will be mutually advantageous to all parties concerned.

Sales as a profession must be characterized by standards of conduct and ethics or by methods of service, and these should be inherent in the profession. It should also have a voice that speaks authoritatively for the profession and fosters the continuing education and development of its practitioners.

Through the achievement of the above, salespeople can truly walk through life with their heads held high, with the firm knowledge and belief that they are ranked as professionals.

And it is the individual salesperson that has to portray this professionalism. It is the salesperson whose standards, ethics, concepts, methods, and dedication win the recognition and appreciation that should be due and accorded to any professional.

James Bryant Connent, a president of Harvard University, really summarized it the best when he said, "The difference between a trade and a profession is that the trader frankly works primarily for pecuniary gain, while the member of a profession professes an art and skill which he places at the public's service for a remuneration, but which skill is truly end in itself. The professional finds his highest rewards in his mastery of his subject, in the pursuit of knowledge for its own sake, and in the contributions that he can make to the promotion of the general welfare."

Yet selling is not an end in itself, but just the beginning. If you think that salespeople only work for themselves and are responsible only to themselves, reflect upon this idea for a moment: a salesperson creates jobs for other people, people who produce, package, and transport the products that are sold. These jobs in turn provide food and shelter for other people who are dependent on their work. Sales produce jobs.

These jobs prevent depression. And who is the top job maker in the country today? None other than salespeople!

Selling thus plays a prime role in each of our lives, and the extent to which we can master and grasp those principles fundamental to selling will determine our success or failure. And this applies to all walks of life and to every profession, whether it is in ministry, medicine, law, or, especially, selling. And while some may have more of a gifted ability to sell than others, the application of the fundamental principles to be set forth will be the determining factor in providing each and every person who has the desire and determination to succeed with the necessary tools to do so.

It becomes obvious, as we delve deeper into the subject of selling, that we are all involved directly in the process of selling something, whether it is ourselves, our ideas, or some product. And only after this concept has been grasped (the idea that we all have something to sell) can we begin to appreciate and understand those fundamentals that are basic to our lives and happiness. Then and only then do we realize that any aspect of selling acquired will lead to a direct return on our individual success. And when these fundamental principles are applied in a manner such that a conscious effort is made to use selling tools instead of being used by them, the importance of selling becomes clear, and sales as a profession can gain the same stature attached to other professions.

And a sale is being made all the time; either you are selling or being sold. The understanding of those principles of sales will not only enable us to perceive when we are trying to be sold to; it also will help us to cope with those attempts to our own advantage.

Each and every one of us has felt the principles of selling applied against us. Selling and salesmanship is a dynamic process, a two-way system of communication. Whenever two people are involved in their interpersonal lives, through business, or through the conveyance of ideas, selling is taking place.

When we are wined and dined and enticed, when we are pitched to (soft or hard), when we are wooed by endorsements or commercials geared to selling us something on television or radio, someone is trying to sell us on something. This means that someone is directing those same principles and fundamentals of selling (to be set forth herein) against us.

An understanding of the principles involved in selling will make us more aware of them as they are being applied against us, as they are being used to sell us. And through this understanding, we can turn those attempts into more productive and rewarding opportunities for ourselves.

Principles of Learning or Changing Behavior

People learn only if they want to. To change their perception, desire, or point of view, you must recognize what their motivations are. Those could include wanting to please a boss, achieve greater success on the job, or gain the satisfaction of learning something new.

The Swiss psychologist, Jean Piaget, developed a ground breaking theory on learning. He coined the term "schema" to describe a set of linked mental representations of the world which is used to understand and respond to situations, which we store and then apply as needed.

A person might want to communicate (what I call the act of selling) an idea, product, feeling/emotion, or desire. The schema for doing this is a stored form of "pattern of behavior" which includes formulating (a) what you want to communicate (pre-approach), (b) defining to whom you want to communicate (approach/prospecting), (c) making your presentation, and (d) closing the deal.

Each time we want to engage in this process, each time we want to make a sale, we retrieve this schema from our memory and apply it to the situation we find ourselves in.

By increasing the complexity and number of these schemata (plural for schema) a person learns. Through the process of assimilation, we use the existing schema to deal with a new situation. Through the process of accommodation, we change our schema (knowledge) to deal with this new situation. Equilibrium is established when we have processed and assimilated our new schema to master our new situation.

Accordingly, if a schema is a unit of knowledge relating one situation to another situation, then nothing can be learned, sold, changed, or communicated until the schema for doing so is developed.

Piaget's theory is that "a schema is a cohesive, repeatable sequence of actions that are tightly connected and governed by a core meaning". This is the basis for the People Business; the idea that sales people can be taught and that, once taught, this training/learning can manifest in new found confidence and ability. We will provide you with this repeatable sequence of actions and their core meaning.

And though Piaget's theories involved children, the dynamics of sales are similar. That similarity being that just as children are a "blank slate", so to the object of our communication, the one to whom we are trying to communicate, sell to, or influence, needs to be taken back to the stage of being a "blank slate" in order to be re-ingrained! We crate dissonance in order to establish equilibrium.

Thus, intelligence is not a fixed, ingrained trait; it is a process which occurs due to interaction and maturation of the schema. It is not the natural born salesman that will win the day, but the trained salesman that follows the principles laid out in this book, that will be sought out and be employable. Assimilation and accommodation require an active learner engaged in active discovery. That is what we are doing here.

For, since no one learns until they have developed a schema to do so, the focus must be on the process; and the process is only initiated by *doing*! It is not enough to just to listen, or to just read, or to just process.

Learning comes about when information received is translated into action. Learning comes about by repetition!

Repetition breeds habit! Habit makes our learning, our schema, automatic. And this automation, this habit, this repetition allows us to exercise the principles that I will outline to you herein; the principles that govern effective sales activities. The result will allows us to engage in more observation of our situation, allowing for better processing of the environment we find ourselves in, leading to greater learning and ability.

So, all of the training, lecturing, and learning will avail naught without active repetition, without the active doing and putting into practice that which we will learn to do.

Furthermore, we can also see that learning is faster and more lasting when you are told the results of your attempt to learn immediately after displaying it. This is the principle of immediate gratification, which results when you are rewarded with a grade, praise, or other form of acknowledgment immediately after demonstrating what you have learned, accomplished, or purchased.

Learning involves practicing, demonstrating, or using what has just been acquired. Listening may help create understanding, but true learning shows up only in behavior. People change their behavior, or learn, only when they can tie the new learning experience, purchase, or idea into the things they already know. All your past experiences will have an effect on and determine what you learn from a new experience.

Which brings us to an important question: how do we motivate someone to take action, to do something, to buy something, or to learn something? A person cannot be forced to "buy/purchase" anything they don't want (or, they don't know they want). But, they can be **persuaded** to do so.

Motivation is the alter ego of persuasion. It is the convincing, the persuading, of someone to feel, act, or want something. And, not *just* the convincing, but the moving of someone to *want* to feel, act, or desire. In other words, the person is brought to believe that it is their volition that propels them to the proposition that you are advocating.

Motivation is getting someone to do something; persuasion is the moving someone to *believe* that it is their own idea, want, need, or desire that they are motivated by. How this is accomplished is an indicator of who is in command of the selling/communication situation.

Motivation is accomplished by the perception of tangible or intangible reward. Discounts, friendship, love, prizes, avoidance/relief from pain, or pleasure are all motivational factors. By using imaginative methods (appeal to character), product information (appeal to reason), and/or appeals to emotion, a "buyer" can be moved to accept something specific for a personal benefit or use that he may not otherwise have wanted or may not otherwise have known to want or need.

How we discover what motivates or persuades someone is a two-step process: it requires problem solving and questioning. Before we can do either, we have to become good listeners.

These are some of the most common motivating factors:

- physical pleasure; avoidance of effort; comfort
- play and relaxation
- esthetic pleasure
- self-esteem, pride, need to feel important; ego striving; urge to achieve; status conscious; willpower
- money gain or acquisitiveness
- romantic or sexual drive; need to be with people
- physical and mental health; physical fitness
- curiosity or desire for new experiences
- the urge to create
- desire for justice; sense of duty; love for others; fear; or caution

Part IV

The Art of Selling

People study three years to become a lawyer, six years to become a physician, and over twelve years to become an astronaut, yet new salespeople go out on the road to sell goods with no basis or training. Their equipment consists of a sample case, a smattering of information about the product or proposition, and a chance to make good. The great majority of salespeople are untrained, unskilled laborers; actual experience is their only school.

Novice salespeople rely on luck and good fortune to see them through to the point where experience takes over. They generally feel like a square peg in a round hole. Yet those who trust to luck progress at a snail's pace. There is no such thing as a square peg in a round hole in the ranks of those who are successful. When successful people find themselves in a round hole, they are round; in a square hole, they are square. Successful people adapt to their surroundings and their demands. They are able to search out for principles and apply them.

This section is intended to analyze and present those principles necessary for a successful selling career and enriched life. As you grasp these principles and gain insight into the inner workings of sales, apply them.

The Making of a Salesperson

1. The Psychology of Selling

The people business, as the name implies, involves people. And since we all are selling something whenever we deal with other people, we must first understand and make use of that branch of science that involves mental and behavioral aspects of people: psychology.

From the study of people, there emerges a psychology of selling, a science that deals with attitude and the effective means of persuading people to change their attitudes and buy the product or adopt the proposition that we want to sell them. The human mind has a strong need for consistency, and a change in attitude is required when faced with an inconsistency, an inconsistency created the moment a salesperson begins to sway a prospect to a particular way of thinking in order to induce them to buy a product or adopt a proposition. The direction and extent to which we can successfully eliminate this inconsistency determines whether we make a sale or not.

To illustrate this point, let's view what happens when Bob Simon walks into Lookwell Clothing Store and is approached by Art, the salesman. Bob and Art have never met before, so they have no association, and each appear neutral to the other.

If Art is an inexperienced or untrained salesman, the encounter might go something like this:

(Art) "Good morning, sir. Can I help you?"

(Mr. Simon) "Yes! I'm looking for a suit."

(Art) "Right this way, sir; these suits are just the thing for you. I think they will look very good on you."

At this point, Art has committed himself. Mr. Simon, on the other hand, might find the suits undesirable by virtue of their price or appearance and thus would tend to hold Art in the same undesirable light or lose respect for Art's suggestion. This would be the end on the sales attempt in the majority of cases, for even if Mr. Simon found a suit that he liked, there would be an inconsistency between his like for the suit and his dislike for the salesman.

If, on the other hand, Art is experienced and more skillful, the encounter would be different.

(Art) "Good morning, my name is Art. Can I help you?"

(Mr. Simon) "Yes, I'm Bob Simon, and I am looking for a suit."

(Art) "Right this way, Mr. Simon. Is there anything in particular that you are looking for? What's your price range?"

By not at once revealing his own preference, Art has allowed Mr. Simon to look over the possibilities and express his taste. When Mr. Simon finds a suit he likes, Art will hasten to agree, thus making Art consistent with Mr. Simon's attitude and way of thinking. If Mr. Simon finds fault with some of the styles, Art will hasten to agree, again making him consistent with his customer. This establishes Art as a man of good taste consonant with Mr. Simon's attitudes.

At this point, Art can use his new position to suggest a suit that might not totally appeal to Mr. Simon, and use this position to change Mr. Simon's mind about it as follows:

(Art) "Mr. Simon, I know that this suit costs slightly more than you wanted to pay, but I think it's just what you are looking for."

(Mr. Simon) "Yes, Art; I think that you are right. I'll take it."

Art has successfully eliminated the inconsistency in Mr. Simon's mind created by the higher cost of the suit and his preference for another style. This resulted in the sale.

Of course, if Art agrees with Mr. Simon's taste, after that taste has already been expressed, this may seem insincere and obvious. If Art is alert and notices a pattern to Mr. Simon's choices, he can make an informed suggestion of another suit. This consistency principle is the basis of the depth theory of selling.

The principle recognized in depth selling is that buyers often approaches the salesperson with a need or want before it is expressed in terms of a specific product or service.

Through conversation, the salesperson can assist buyers in exploring and focusing on their needs and can also explore their own inventory to determine if they will satisfy them. This interchange of ideas leads to a clarification of the buyer's problem(s) and also leads to an understanding of how the salesperson can help solve them.

The depth theory recognizes the fact that every customer and every selling situation is different. It also places a special emphasis on the salesperson's abilities in customer analysis, solving problems, and making decisions. This theory is more customer oriented than seller oriented, since it considers not only the customer's needs and wants but also the seller's needs and wants. Communication between the salesperson and the customer is an essential part of this theory.

Depth selling accomplishes three major objectives: It helps salespeople understand themselves; without this understanding, they cannot solve the buying problem of others. It helps them to understand the needs and wants of others. It helps develop their skills as decision makers and problem solvers.

Most people generally tend to buy for emotional reasons rather than rational ones. Of course, rationality has a part in the decision process, but emotional motives generally play a greater part in inducing someone to buy a product or agree with a new proposition.

Emotions are very complex and difficult to isolate and classify. Many emotional motives are involved in creating the need, want, or desire to buy something. Here are some of the most common emotional buying motives:

Physical Pleasure, Avoidance of Effort, or Comfort

Humans are animals, and people naturally live most of their lives on a physical level. They require food, drink, sleep, and a temperature that's not too hot nor too cold. Most people spend a great deal of effort in acquiring these basic necessities. Others are able to satisfy these with less effort and then go on from there to acquire other desirable things. This urge is basic and accounts for the purchase of food, cars, soft mattresses, shelter, clothes, and conveniences for the home or office. Washing machines, vacuum cleaners, dishwashers, elevators, inside toilets, cars with automatic transmissions, and air conditioning are examples of things we value because they satisfy this particular type of urge. The absence of pleasure causes us discomfort or pain. Perhaps this discomfort or pain is merely the necessity of putting forth physical or mental effort, but to most of us, effort is akin to pain. As Mark Twain is quoted as saying, "Men are as lazy as they dare to be, and some of them are mighty daring." Attaining pleasure and avoiding effort are very fundamental and powerful buying motives.

Play, Relaxation, and Aesthetic Pleasure

Playing provides a form of physical and sometimes aesthetic pleasure. Leisure time for play has expanded with the use of power-driven machinery to replace human labor. This drive for play is quite basic in all animals; the desire for play seems quite strong and is manifested in many ways in our society. (Note the successful stores decorated in make-believe decor: erect a playhouse and customers will come play with you.) Witness the success of many nonsense advertising campaigns: for instance, a white knight comes charging across the scene. A dove flies into the kitchen, while the

Jolly Green Giant goes, "Ho, ho, ho," and Charley the Tuna bemoans his lack of breeding.

This play theory leads to some rather useful thoughts for salespeople. Obviously, people who want to play need playmates. Many successful salespeople owe their fortune to their abilities as playmates. Successful executives have a limited number of people they can play with. The people in their own organization are usually excluded because of managerial considerations. The salesperson may be able to play just the right role for such an executive who wants to escape to the golf course or go on a short vacation, which may develop into a lasting relationship for the salesperson that would never have been achieved otherwise. But the key fact to remember is that people must play. The problem for salespeople is to discover just what form that play takes in their customer's behavior pattern.

Self-Esteem, Pride, the Need to Feel Important

All of us want to be appreciated, to be complimented, and to feel important. Salespeople cannot afford to forget this motive. Indeed, many salespeople assert that this is the most powerful of all buying motives. Not only must people feel they are of some importance, they also crave recognition of this from others.

An appreciation of this very human trait enables salespeople to use indirect methods in place of the often offensive direct method. It's more tactful to use indirection, which recognizes the customer's desire to feel important. We therefore merely suggest instead of dictate.

In the long run, people like to make their own decisions, at least in matters that concern them intimately. We all resent backseat drivers, so salespeople try to present their views so prospects can buy without feeling that they've been forced into it. They must be made to feel that they did the buying, that they made a wise decision of their own free will.

Smart salespeople don't do all the talking; they cater to the prospect's desire to feel important. They learn to listen to their prospect's opinions, acknowledging them with courteous deference. They are careful of how they tell a story; avoiding showing off, acting like the final authority on the subject, or telling the prospect something they did not know. They shun introductory clauses such as "Maybe you never thought of this angle, but ..." or "You probably didn't know this before, but ...".

Instead, they are quick to impute their own ideas to the prospect or to someone else. They say, "As you mentioned a few minutes ago ...", knowing the prospect will more readily accept the idea.

The common statement "See what I mean?" irritates many listeners, who mentally react, *"Of course I do; do you think I'm a moron?"* The wise salesperson uses praise judiciously. It costs so little and pays such huge dividends. Also in passing, it might be observed that a person enjoys being complimented on some trait that is not frequently noticed, such as when a beautiful girl is told she has a wonderful mind. Someone said, "Make a man like himself a little bit better, and he will henceforth like you very much."

Imitation

Most people imitate others in the purchase of certain things with the idea that by doing so, they are showing themselves superior to those who do not follow the fashion. To this extent, this motive is akin to the urge for self-importance. Salespeople can utilize this buying motive in the sale of many things, but they must always be certain that the person they suggest the prospect imitate is viewed favorably by them. Only then will being like them satisfactorily inflate the buyer's ego.

Money Gain

This buying motive has two parts. The first one prompts the buyer to make money; the other emphasizes more strongly the savings of money. That is, the first is positive in its implication, whereas the latter is negative. Buyers of the first class are willing to spend money to make more money. They have big vision, and the saving of money is not their aim. There is nothing of the penurious or the miser in them. The making of money is more of a game, a competitive sport, than mere accumulation of wealth.

These people are more willing to take a chance with their money than are those of the saver type.

Salespeople appeal to buyers of the second class, the savers, differently. These people save rather than make money. Their outlook is narrower; they are more cautious. With people of little means, the savings appeal can be explosive. Just the illusion of a saving can bring forth a sale.

Other basic buying urges include the desire for possessions and the urge to hoard or collect. People seem to have an urge to call things theirs. Also, the romantic and sexual drives should be appealed to. These are related to the desire to be with people. Health, physical fitness, curiosity, a desire for a new experience, the urge to create, a desire for justice, or a sense of duty or love for others are all extremely strong buying motives that emotionally influence people to make a purchase.

Good salespeople consider all of these psychological principles and emotional appeals and incorporate them into their presentations (which we will get into shortly); during the course of the presentation, they appeal to all of those buying motives. This should reach a crescendo during the close, to the extent that they will have generated the commitment for the customer to buy the product or accept the proposition.

Characteristic and Attributes Necessary for Successful Selling

Everyone is inclined to be impressed by people who know their proposition thoroughly, believe in it enthusiastically, and honestly wish others to know about and benefit by it. The impressions we make will not only enable us to do things, it will largely relieve us of the necessity of making claims. The claims that customers make about our ability, honesty, and conscientiousness are stronger than any claims we would dare put forth ourselves.

Therefore, our success is based on the impressions we make upon people with whom we come in contact for the first time and the degree to which we build upon, live up to, or fall short of the original impression we made. And this impression is conveyed in two ways: physical and mental. Both are necessary and equally as important.

Physical Characteristics

Good health is of great importance; it is the foundation upon which our physical and mental qualities are built. The chief factors that contribute to good health are proper diet, exercise, sleep, and medical care. Diet is important, as everyone must be careful of what and when they eat. In selling, the strain and bustle of the job often leads to irregular eating habits.

Exercise: Most salespeople get some exercise on the job, but most of them need additional regular exercise to stay in good health. Certain sports are recommended because they are not tiring for those in reasonably good health; these include volleyball, bowling, tennis, golf, swimming, and baseball. Skating and jogging are becoming very popular and are excellent forms of exercise.

Sleep: Without adequate sleep, salespeople cannot be in prime condition to serve their customers. They should relax for five or ten minutes several times during the day. A brief rest does much to restore waning energy and enthusiasm.

Posture: Good posture contributes to good health and adds to your overall physical appearance. Poor posture can quickly detract from an otherwise attractive appearance. Failure to stand erect with the body well balanced on their feet makes you look slouchy and awkward. Your good posture gives the impression that you are confident in yourself and are successful in your work.

Mental Characteristics

Enthusiasm: This is not false enthusiasm, the affected, loud-voiced, table-pounding type of aggressive enthusiasm; that's counterfeit. It's phony. And it's easily discovered by an intelligent buyer. By enthusiasm, I'm talking about a genuine calm enthusiasm. It comes from a confidence in yourself, in your company, and in your product; but most importantly, in the rightness, the importance, the necessity of your product.

Sincerity: Professional salespeople never find it necessary to resort to evasions, misleading statements, exaggerated claims, or double dealing. When they are wrong, they must readily admit to it, but when they don't know an answer, they should admit that they don't know and come back with the answer later. Research it, look it up, discover it, then answer it. You can't fake sincerity; people are too smart today. It stands out; when you appear to be insincere, it makes everything else you say suspect to doubt and suspicion. Cleverness or shrewdness isn't necessary. Keep it simple; keep it basic; be honest and sincere.

Loyalty: What can you say about loyalty? You can't possibly hope to belittle a product or company without belittling yourself at the same time, especially if you work for that company or are connected to that product in some way.

About the best quote concerning loyalty comes from Elbert Hubbard, who said, "If you work for a man, in heaven's name, work for him. If he pays wages that supply you with bread and butter, *work* for him, speak well of him, think well of him, stand by him and stand by the institution he represents. If in a pinch, an ounce of loyalty is worth a pound of cleverness. If you must vilify, condemn and eternally disparage then resign your position and, when you are outside, damn to your heart's content. But I pray to you, as long as you are part of an institution do not condemn it. Not that you will injure the institution, not that, but when you disparage the concern of which you are a part you also disparage yourself."

Initiative: A small part of the work of a salesperson is routine. It's prescribed by policy and by demands of the job. But salespeople who are distinguished as winners achieve their success based on the amount of initiative they apply in selling. Mediocrity is filled by those who do only what they must and only what they are told to do.

Salesmanship is more individual; it allows you to explore new ideas and better ways of doing things as you practice initiative without violating company policy or turning against sound business practices.

Dare to be different, be innovative, be imaginative, and you'll see how more challenging, more rewarding, more fun your work can be.

Perseverance: This is stick-to-itiveness, or as Bert Schlain likes to call it, "a high frustration tolerance." A salesperson can't afford to become discouraged because of turn-downs or setbacks, as these are an inherent part of selling. It's going to happen in anything you do, the point of expectation. You have to expect occasional disappointment and sometimes defeat. But the key is to not let it get you down or keep you down. Using a very old cliché, when the going gets tough, the tough get going, and it's just as true today.

Worry can kill you. It drains you of energy; it keeps you stagnant. Psychologically, it can make you quite ill. Most of the things we worry about never happen, anyway. Worrying over things that have already happened is useless because you can't change them, and worrying about things which are to come is senseless, since they haven't happened. You have to learn to rise above a defeat or disappointment. You have to develop a perspective of things. Stick to your task, keep your goal in sight, and above all, forge ever ahead.

Attitude: A professional attitude is a state of mind. It goes beyond mere acting or behavior. Attitude, more than anything else, will determine your success. If you have that conviction, that belief, that deep sincere certainty that you are a professional, you can't help but look and feel like one and think and behave like one. And when you do this, you will be amazed how people will begin accepting you at your own evaluation.

If you don't think highly of yourself, if you have a bad attitude about yourself, how do you expect other people to believe in you, to have faith in you? How can you cause others to buy into your proposition, when you don't have the courage of your own convictions?

When a person starts from the position of knowing that he has the skill, the ability to succeed; that he has a story to communicate; a purpose to make a presentation, to teach, to enlighten, to establish, a reason to want to communicate, not just make a sale, then sales will flow in abundance. When a person has the confidence of knowing that what he is doing, and how he is doing it is beneficial, good, and just, then he will exude that confidence no matter what the environment or outcome.

The correct attitude can guide you on your way to success. It can free you to function as a professional. And, as such, it can carry you along your path to attain the goals you have set for yourself.

Honesty: Salespeople must be honest with themselves, with their employer, and most importantly, with their customer. Honesty is the fairness and straightforwardness of conduct. Being honest with yourself means putting forth your best effort and doing a full day's work every day. This honesty should bring personal satisfaction. Stealing from an employer or collecting payments for services not performed is flagrantly dishonest. Honesty in dealing with customers is the foundation of long term salesperson-customer relationships, and there is a direct connection between honesty with yourself and honesty with your employer. Honesty with the employer requires nothing less than 100 percent integrity.

Responsibility: Responsibility is carrying out the promises you made and seeing through of the job. An unreliable person can destroy a sound business relationship almost as much as a dishonest one. The unreliable person shows no respect for the interests and rights of others. Sometimes, a salesperson makes an appointment with a customer and then fails to keep it. Such conduct shows a lack of responsibility.

Courage: Courage is the mental and moral strength that enables you to withstand danger, fear, or difficulty. Salespeople need courage because they must continuously contact and influence other people, many of whom are strangers, whose likes and dislikes are unknown to them. Courageous salespeople will stick to their job even when everything seems to be going against them. Such courage depends upon the salesperson's self-confidence, belief in the product, and commitment to the firm. It requires perseverance and foresight to realize that troubles are temporary and that you have within yourself a strength reserve upon which you can draw.

Imagination and Showmanship: Imagination enables people to form mental images of things that are not before them. In selling, imagination is the ability to see an article in use and to visualize new uses for it and new ways to combine it with other products. Selling really has more to do with selling the use of an article than with selling the article itself. This requires the salesperson to know about the article and also have a vivid imagination. Showmanship is a form of applied imagination. It is useful and sometimes very necessary in selling. It is a knack for dramatization, the ability to present something to the customer in an exciting way.

Ambition: Ambition is the ever-present desire to achieve something. It is the drive that makes us work to attain our goals. It asserts itself mainly in the achievement of small victories because success usually comes not from one great achievement but from a multitude of small jobs, done well. In sales, ambition may appear as an attempt to break previous sales records or to outdo everyone else. Ambition, however, should always be subordinate to honesty.

Adaptability: Adaptability is the quality of being able to adjust or conform to a new set of circumstances and to different types of people. It can be both an intellectual and a social characteristic. Since selling situations never remain constant, salespeople must be able to adapt easily. Adaptability requires consideration of four points: First of all, you cannot change people; they change only when they want to. Second, you must change what you can and accept what you cannot change. Third, you must try to change yourself first, and fourth, you must be positive in your mental outlook.

To prepare for possible future changes in position, a salesperson should make every effort to retain flexibility of mind and also of action.

Language/Speech

And while all of the above are important, the most critical attribute that salespeople must have is speech. For salespeople, it is not only what they say but how they say it that enables them to gain and hold the customer's attention.

The function of a good selling voice is first of all to carry a message to the prospect; second, to keep the prospect's attention centered on the sales message; and third, to create a feeling of confidence in the salesperson. Some principles of speaking effectively are to speak distinctly, speak with moderate speed, speak reasonably loudly, emphasize key words and phrases, vary the pitch of the voice, speak in a conversational tone, and most importantly, speak sincerely.

Language is one of the salesperson's most important tools, for it is the chief means of conveying information to a prospective customer about the product or service being sold. If salespeople cannot speak clearly and confidently, they cannot sell. No matter how fine their personality, no matter how sincere their interest in their product, and no matter how impressive their sales demonstration is, if they cannot speak clearly and confidently, they just will not sell.

The ability to use verbal language correctly and forcefully is one of the most necessary qualifications for salespeople. They must be able to express themselves clearly in written language, but because verbal skills are more important than written skills to most salespeople, they must be able to speak expressively and enthusiastically and skillfully.

Yet a large vocabulary will be of little value to salespeople unless they can choose the proper words to use in their sales talks. Words should be appropriate to the article being sold and should be selected with the customer in mind. If salespeople use words that prospective customer cannot understand, they will probably not convince them to buy. A great problem in choosing the proper words is the use of technical terms; words commonly used by members of one trade or profession may be unknown to other people.

It is always dangerous to use technical terms in describing an article to someone who is not familiar with them. Salespeople may use the precise vocabulary of a trade in talking with others belonging to this trade, but they should never try to show off their technical knowledge.

Another problem in choosing words is the emotional impact and association some words have. Words and phrases are often loaded; they create emotional responses in the listener that may either be favorable or unfavorable. For instance, most people associate the word *cheap* not only with low price but with poor quality, so the wise salesperson substitutes the word *inexpensive.* Salespeople should use short words rather than long words in sales talks because short words are more clearly understood, and they are often more forceful than longer words. Clever speakers vary their use of long and short words purely to attract attention.

In general, slang should be avoided. It is usually inexact and careless language that goes out of date quickly, and it often gives a bad impression of the speaker. The consistent use of slang decreases a salesperson's command of effective verbal language. The use of incorrect grammar is harmful for several reasons. First of all, poor grammar immediately lowers the salesperson in the estimation of customers, especially those who are well educated. Second, incorrect grammar may give the prospect a poor impression of the firm that the salesperson represents.

Also, incorrect grammar is likely to draw the customer's attention from what the salespeople are saying to how they are saying it, and anything that takes the customer's attention from the selling message reduces the chances of making a sale. But most importantly, incorrect grammar may garble the intended idea and lead to misunderstanding.

Too many salespeople have developed mannerisms that are distracting to customers, mannerisms of gesture, expression, posture, and so on. You may consider such mannerisms unimportant, but if they irritate or distract a customer, they can most assuredly destroy any image that you are trying to project and result in the loss of a sale. Mannerisms that should be avoided include continually clearing your throat; twirling your hat; thumping on furniture with a finger or a pencil, twitching your head, arms, or legs; and tapping on the floor with your foot.

Equally as important and apart from the knowledge that you must have of your product, you should also be knowledgeable and well versed in subjects that are completely unrelated to business but that are equally vital to your image as a professional. A salesperson must be conversant with world, national, and local politics. Salespeople have to be familiar with what's going on in their community; they must be abreast of social affairs and civic functions. They should know something about sports, both amateur and professional, and they must have at least a limited knowledge of music, art, and literature. Salespeople have to raise their intellectual and conversation level to a high position.

You must possess all of the above qualities in order to achieve a level of success in accordance with your goals and desires. And bear in mind most salespeople are trained and not born; all these qualities can be acquired and mastered, with diligence and a desire to better yourself. These are qualities that are only attained by a deliberate and conscious effort to improve the quality of your life.

Salespeople should recognize that moods do exist and that they are constantly changing. They should attempt to plan their work around their moods, as long as they can do this without harming their productivity. On some days, they are better equipped mentally to take a long trip and call on a large number of customers, to deal with a difficult customer who has a problem that requires ingenuity to solve, or to calculate costs of a proposed installation involving a great many variable factors.

Knowing that temporary depression will pass and be replaced by more positive moods permits salespeople to react constructively to this and plan for more effective use of their time.

Training a Salesperson

Order takers canvass for people who want to buy; salespeople try to make everyone they call on want to buy. Order takers accepts the situations they find; salespeople create a special situation to suit their purpose.

The development of salespeople to achieve their full potential is contingent on their ability to establish just such a selling situation characterized by the following:

a. their ability to organize their selling and themselves
b. their capacity to think creatively
c. their aptitude in understanding their own product or proposition as well as their competition's, in order to effectively answer objections
d. their ability to present their case to any potential customer who will give them the opportunity to make a presentation

A potential customer is anyone you are selling (or trying to sell) a product or proposition. A customer is anyone who will listen to your presentation, who uses or needs your product, or who has expressed an interest in your product or proposition.

Ask any salesperson if they have ever made a sale to someone who originally stated that they would not buy and the answer would be a resounding yes. In fact, the ones who protest the most are usually those who buy with the least amount of resistance. Hence, it is smart to treat all prospects as though they were valued customers.

The aim should not merely be to make a sale but rather to make a customer. This attitude has a suggestive force, tending toward both the sale and the customer.

Time is the most valuable asset of salespeople. Time can either be their enemy or their friend, depending on how it's used; time can be a willing servant for a benevolent master, or it can be a rebellious servant to who wastes it. The thing that sinks most salespeople, one of their greatest faults, is the fact that they are unorganized; they go about gathering their prospects, setting up appointments, presenting their proposition or product in a helter-skelter sort of way, all the while wasting a considerable amount of time that if put to good use could increase their sales and make them considerably more successful.

Salespeople must be orderly, systematic, and organized in their approach to selling. As previously stated, this is one of the hallmarks of professionalism. This organization leads to a four-step approach to selling, which will bring us to our final objective: securing the order.

These four steps are as follows:

1. Preapproach
2. Approach
3. Presentation
4. Close and departure

And although they are listed separately, they are all interdependent and each must be used in conjunction with the others.

Preapproach

In the preapproach step, we are striving for product knowledge. This consists of investigation and research not only in our own product or proposition, but in our competition's product, as well. Everyone is inclined to be impressed by those who know their proposition thoroughly, believe in it enthusiastically, and honestly wish others to know about it.

Understanding the nature of what you are selling can never be overstressed and must never be underemphasized. Salespeople must create specialized situations; they have to put prospects in the market who didn't feel that way before they started talking. And the only way of so doing is to possess a firm understanding of the product or proposition they are trying to sell. For only through a firm grasp of the product or proposition can they explain it to the point of making someone else desire it. You can't expect to sell something which you know nothing about.

And more than just a cursory understanding is necessary. The prospect will invariably ask questions, which many times will positively amaze you. It is necessary for salespeople to answer those questions honestly and effectively based on a firm understanding of their product or proposition.

Salespeople should be able to give the buyer the benefit of their wider experience and greater knowledge, convincing them that what they are selling is best adapted to meet the prospect's needs.

Salespeople have to be trained to develop an insight into their own product. They must be aware of the steps their product goes through before it reaches its final completion. They must be aware of certain facts pertaining to the raw materials used in the manufacture of the product: who supplies them, the physical and chemical properties, and their strength, all of which are important to the degree that these properties affect the quality and life of the end product.

Every step in the manufacture of the product is important, from unloading the raw materials to delivering the finished product. The salesperson should thoroughly understand the method of transportation.

It becomes apparent that there are differences in quality and price among competitive products. If customers say, "Oh, all products are alike," you can give yourself a competitive edge by being aware of the various quality controls that are used in your company's production process.

Specifications, tolerances of raw materials, different steps used in the making of your product, the rate of perfection, and the controls used all enable you to show buyers why they should choose your product as opposed to a competitive one.

Further, you should be aware of your entire product line. To be a complete salesperson, you have to know your complete line. There's no way you can get around that. Salespeople must be aware of all the products their company produces as well as their particular characteristics, purposes, or properties that make it right for a given prospect, a specific problem, or a special situation. Don't get into the habit of selling only the easy items, the ones that you like best. Sell your complete line.

But it's just as important to have a firm understanding of your own product or proposition, as your competitor's product. To know that one product is better than another, you must know about the others. It follows that in order to effectively answer objections to other products, you must have a firm understanding of those other products.

Salespeople should know if there is a product equal to theirs, if it's better or worse, and if it is worse, in what ways. They must know how competitive products are different and how that affects their value; they must learn how they can highlight the superior features of their product to offset the competition. They should know the competition's products so well that they can quickly recognize them and identify their maker. They should be able to pick their own product from a group of similar products. For only this way will they be in a position to look for and find the demonstrable differences between their product and those of the competition.

Now, these differences can be in raw materials, production methods, quality controls, completeness of line, shipping policies, prices, or a combination of all of these factors. The essential question that will be asked by a customer is, "Why should I buy from you rather than from another company?" The extent to which these differences can be seen, felt, measured, and figured out with the prospect, the extent to which they can be shown and proved through the use of product knowledge, will determine whether you attain your ultimate goal: making the sale.

Why Is a Preapproach Necessary?

The most important, and yet limited, commodity that salespeople have is their time. The preapproach enables them to make a quick start every day, saving time by knowing where they are going and who they are meeting with. This allows them to plan what they are going to say and how they are going to say it.

Equally important, prospects are in a better mood, as they find their time spent more profitably with salespeople who care about their time as well as their own.

Approach

With the right approach, salespeople can secure an opportunity to present their product to prospective customers. A correct approach means more than merely inducing people to notice that you wish to sell them something; it involves getting them to set aside other matters they may be occupied with and concentrate their thoughts on your proposition or product. You must assume that your proposition or product is so important that they must hear all about it.

Salespeople must be ready at all times to present their product or proposition since they are subject to the schedule of the customer. However, at no time should they be effusive or submissive. As they attempt to secure an appointment or opportunity to demonstrate their product, they must maintain their forcefulness and control as they lead the customer in the direction they want.

Bear in mind that the prospect doesn't owe you an interview or anything else, for that matter. You're asking for a portion of the prospect's valuable time. If he's good enough to grant it to you, then you should feel professionally obligated to make the time spent worthwhile. The chief reason in making an appointment is to avoid wasting time on a cold call to your prospect's office to find out that he's out, that he's in conference, or that he's too busy to see you. Setting a specific appointment not only saves hours of waiting time, it also makes the demonstration phase of the interview a lot easier, since the prospect knows your name, at least, and knows why you're coming. It also means that the prospect has set aside some time, hopefully free from interruptions, to give you his undivided attention.

And this is exactly the best you can expect: an opportunity to present your proposal or proposition in a positive atmosphere, where your prospect can devote his full attention to what you have to say.

When using the telephone to make an appointment, make the message brief, as brief as possible. Make sure your voice is pleasant, conversational, and relaxed. Know exactly what you're going to say. Remember that what you're trying to do is get an interview, to get an appointment. Handle the situation carefully. Be honest and straightforward, don't misrepresent, and above all, don't disclose your entire presentation on the phone. In making the appointment, present a choice between appointment times. Give him the choice between two positives; don't leave it up to him to say no. The standard approach is "May I call on you at 4:30 Wednesday or 11:30 Thursday? If that's not convenient, when is the best day to call on you? Is Tuesday or Wednesday a better time, day or night?"

To give an example, allow me to draw upon a technique that I used while working for *Encyclopedia Britannica*. The names of our prospects were obtained by cards the prospect mailed into our office, requesting information by way of a booklet we had. In most cases, the prospect expected to receive information by mail; they were usually surprised when a representative called on them. In order to secure the appointment, I would call on the phone and say:

"Hello, Mr. Jones, I'm with *Encyclopedia Britannica*. We received a request for information from you, and I am calling to determine the most convenient time to present you with this information. Would tomorrow be fine, or is the next day better for you?"

By presenting the prospect with the choice of two positives, I do not allow him to say no or claim that there is no good time to see me. If he selects one of the choices, I proceed to do the same thing with the time. However, if he selects neither day or interposes an objection to seeing me, I proceed as follows:

"Mr. Jones, I realize that you are very busy; however, I'm only asking for twenty to thirty minutes of your time to show you our program. I'm sure you'll feel that time to be well invested for your future and the future of your family. So is the morning or evening better for you? [When he selects one, I continue as follows.] Fine, I'll see you Tuesday evening at six o'clock."

I would continue in this manner until the appointment was confirmed. As can be seen, the prospect was led and controlled to my desired goal. This can be done effectively when tact and tolerance are used. Under no circumstance should salespeople become upset if the prospect cannot meet at the time they want. Salespeople must be flexible and, above all, persistent.

It's always easier to set a definite time and date to make your presentation. The approach to getting an appointment is usually very direct and very honest. It follows something similar to this: "Mr. Prospect, I've got some information that I believe would be in the best interests of your business [or "I have something which I believe you will find worth considering"]. Could you give me about thirty minutes, let's say ten o'clock Wednesday, or perhaps two o'clock would be better?" Using this same trend, you can even interject a hint at a specific benefit that your idea might produce: cost savings, profits, greater volume, whatever benefits that might be derived from this product.

And remember, once this appointment has been made, by all means, keep it. Be there ahead of time. Don't keep the customer, your prospect, waiting for you. Your appointment is binding on you. The customer is setting aside a chunk of time for you; don't make him wait for you, as he will lose respect for you. If you waste his time, he will waste your time. It's also bad for your professional image. If, for some reason, you are unable to keep your appointment, call him and tell him. Preferably, tell him so he has enough time to reschedule the appointment. When you call him up to break the appointment, be honest with him and don't make excuses. Remember, he's probably heard most of them already. Be frank and sincere, and offer an explanation; don't just tell him you can't make it. Tell him why you can't make it. He has a right to know, and that will determine whether he reschedules or not.

In making cold calls, be prepared to sell yourself as well as sell the interview. Also, be prepared to sell those points to others, namely the receptionist, secretary, or assistant before finally getting in to see your prospect face-to-face. The challenges that you face depend on what you're selling and who you're calling on. If you are going to sell cold, remember the twofold selling objective: Selling yourself and selling the interview.

In selling yourself, remember that when you approach the prospect for the first time, you could be an unwelcome intruder on his time. Some prospects may take one look and make up their minds negatively about you. Others could be a little more open-minded. That is why it's important that your appearance and grooming are professional and that your manner is such that when you approach prospects, you do so with confidence and with a smile and secure in the knowledge that you're trying to help them. Don't be nervous, don't be hesitant, and don't be worried about the reception you're going to receive.

And after you've sold yourself, you then have to sell the interview. Remember that the best chance for success in making a sale is a situation in which you sit down with prospects and have their undivided attention. Therefore, your approach should be aimed at gaining an interview with those conditions. As noted previously, in order to get to your prospect, you may have to go through a receptionist, secretary, assistant, or someone who screens the prospect's calls.

Bear in mind that in most instances, the person you're trying to reach is very busy, especially if you're calling on him at his office. He is usually busy with calls and correspondence, to the extent that these calls are usually screened by a secretary or assistant. In order to get through them to the prospect, you have to turn them to your way of thinking. You have to put them on your side.

Dealing with a receptionist presents the biggest problem to many salespeople. They tend to regard receptionists as enemies, but they're an obstacle or hurdle that you have to push out of the way. But if you handle the receptionist professionally, if you regard her as an asset, instead of an obstacle, you would find her to be a very beneficial aid who could save you time and assist you in smoothing your way to see the people you want.

When you're dealing with receptionists, be friendly, honest, and sincere. Don't try to bluff or bluster your way around them. Remember, people are doing this to her all the time; she's probably immune to it. Don't use evasion, trickery, or lies to get by her. The worst thing you could do would be to try to get through her under false pretenses or by being belligerent or aggressive.

Remember that the receptionist is there for a specific purpose, and she has her job to do. She's acting under orders from her boss. Her job is to screen the people. You have to work with her; you have to tell her who you are and who you're representing. Very briefly, but in a very convincing manner, state the nature of your product and have her work for you. She knows a lot about the company. She knows a lot about the way to get in to see the very people you want to see, and more often than not, she can give you exact information as to the mood or receptiveness of the person you're trying to see at that time. If you handle the receptionist right, then she can contribute very greatly to your cause and help you get to see the person you want to see.

Dealing with a secretary is similar to dealing with a receptionist. She is there for a specific reason. Especially in a large company, the executive you want to see is usually protected by a secretary. You have to go through the secretary in order to get to the person you want. She can help you or, by the same token, hinder your efforts in getting to see the person you want. Depending on how you handle her, she can aid you, or she can be an obstacle. Remember that she works very closely with the person you're trying to see, your prospect or customer. Be mindful that the suggestions she makes will be listened to and acted upon by her boss.

When you do meet her, do so warmly, with a smile. Don't speak to her as someone beneath you, as someone inferior to you, but as an equal. Tell her the nature of your business. She can tell you what to look for, what your prospect likes, and what he's most likely to be receptive to. She can tell you when the best time to approach him is, when he's most likely to see a salesman, and when he may not be in the mood to see a salesman. She can tell you something about her boss as a person, his likes and dislikes, and she can aid you very much in getting an appointment with him.

As stated previously, the purpose of, or the concept behind, the approach phase of selling is to create an atmosphere conducive to the presentation of your proposition or product. The best method would be in a face-to-face meeting with your prospect, during a previously confirmed appointment.

Remember when you're making the appointment that up to now the buyer has gotten along without you or your product fairly well. If he suffered in any way through not having it, he probably doesn't realize it. And if he does, he is not sure that your product will relieve his suffering.

Remember, too, that you're going to upset his entire way of thinking, his composure, and his complacency when you attempt to sell him. Take care that you do it gently, with understanding and a delicate sensitivity to his feelings, his moods, his responses, and his reactions. Don't rush headlong into an outpouring of your sales story, without pausing for breath.

Take care in what you say. Remember, you are not making the proposition; you are not presenting him yet. You are merely trying to get in to see him. Don't use all your ammunition up. Use only as much as needed to get the appointment.

You are asking the prospect to devote his full attention to you, so assure yourself that the time is most conducive to this end. Don't ask for attention as a favor. Salespeople should always suggest that they are rendering a service to their customers. Don't ask for attention; attract it. Yet never resort to cheap trickery in order to secure attention, as you may find that this instills a level of contempt in the product and the salesperson, which may be difficult if not impossible to overcome.

In the approach, the salesperson must not try to make the sale yet. Although you may give your entire presentation then and there, you must remember that your objective at this point is merely to secure the opportunity to present your proposition. In so doing, you must be ever conscious not to give out more information than is necessary to secure the interview. You must leave some mystery to the proposition; for if not, if the prospect is totally aware of the product, he would have no need to listen to your presentation. There are two main goals that we should strive for in the approach phase:

a. overcome the instinctive antagonism a person has to being sold
b. arousing the customer's curiosity and interest so that he sets aside time to listen to your presentation

And if these two goals are achieved, then you will have created an opportunity conducive to present your product.

Presentation

The presentation is the key to success in any endeavor. Particularly important is that you understand your audience and style your presentation to the goal that you desire: closing the sale!

Your presentation can be memorized or said by route; it can be structured or unstructured (customized to your particular audience); or be so canned that you do all of the talking. In either case, you must be certain to include all of the points necessary to establish the need and provide for its satisfaction.

Using visual aids will help to keep you on track and provide for a degree of showmanship, attracting and maintaining attention.

Any memorized or structured presentation must allow for the ability to customize it to suit your particular audience, and must be adaptable such that the narrative can be changed as required.

Be careful to recognize your prospect's perception. Failure to establish need by a disorganized presentation or by a monotonous tone that renders the presentation uninteresting or boring can be fatal.

Be enthusiastic, but not pushy or arrogant. There is very fine line between pressure and enthusiasm. Be firm, and make your case with skill and deliberateness; but don't poison the atmosphere by attitude or smugness.

Provide enough information to make your case, but never more than is necessary. Weigh carefully your words and their effect on your efforts. Continually make adjustments and corrections.

And, eliminate distractions from the beginning by establishing the optimum surroundings, being mindful of potential problems posed by TV's, Phones, etc.

The presentation is perhaps the single most important phase of the sale. (Note: The words *demonstration* and *presentation* will be used interchangeably throughout in referring to that phase of selling in which you are face-to-face with customers, trying to sell them your product or proposition.) During this phase, you attempt to demonstrate your product, with the resulting aim being to stimulate the desire for the product or proposition and to arouse an impulse to purchase it.

Arousing interest means connecting the product or proposition with an already existing interest. This is done by showing customers how it will contribute to the satisfaction of their needs or desires. With the use of suggestion and logical reasoning throughout the presentation, the salesperson attempts to create a desire for that product. When people are convinced of the desirability of the product, they can be led to see that the satisfaction gained is commensurate with the expenditure involved and is therefore reasonable. No matter how high the price may seem (if it is reasonable), the salesperson must be ready to show that it is really low in comparison with the benefit it will provide. Price becomes secondary.

Salespeople must be able to diagnose the impression they are making on the customer's mind. They must feel out the customer to see when it's the proper time to attempt a close. When dealing with customers, always remember that you're dealing with individuals, living, sensitive people who are unique in personality and emotional makeup. They have their likes and dislikes, their fears and ambitions. They have their own value on things and react to words differently from any other person.

It's important that you treat these people as individuals. Don't try to categorize them. Don't try to stereotype them into a role you think they fit because of looks, income bracket, education, or anything else. Treat them as individuals. Remember that as individuals, they are also going to have their own special mixture of reasons and emotions for buying things; very rarely does a person rely on logic alone in making a purchase. Most decisions to buy are influenced by emotion; emotion of the time and of the mood the customer is in.

Customers will buy from you if they like you, if they trust you, if they respect you, and most important of all, if they believe in you. This is why it is so very important for you to conduct yourself as a professional and to use a professional approach in dealing with your customer.

Moreover, since a customer buys on emotion, be aware of approaches that appeal directly to these emotions. Those motives that could be appealed to would be profit or gain, achievement of personal prestige or recognition, a desire to enlighten oneself or to enhance one's image, or to feel important.

Be cognizant of the fact that fear, which is a negative motive, is a very delicate and dangerous motive to elicit in your customer. Fear can be implied by pointing out the benefits of your product in such a way as to imply that customers will lose out if they don't have it. A common rebuttal used in the close, especially a favorite of insurance salespeople, is when the prospect says, "I cannot afford to buy insurance," the salesperson shoots back, "You can't afford not to buy it."

But in eliciting fear, be very, very careful; you're treading dangerously on an emotion that might have disastrous effects in terms of whether you make the sale or not.

Demonstration

The sales presentation should consist of the following points:

- A short, convincing demonstration. Keep the presentation moving smoothly and at a crisp pace; don't allow yourself to become bogged down with a lot of superfluous talk. Abbreviate and eliminate all but the salient aspects of the product or proposition. Convey your own feelings.
- Do not show fear, haste, or uncertainty; know your product well, be confident, and relax.
- Be the master of the interview and know what you are going to say; know how to say it.
- Know where to close; know when to stop selling and when to start closing: at the peak of interest.
- Adapt the demonstration to the customer.
- Use showmanship and persuasion.

With these points in mind, you are now ready to demonstrate your product and make your sale. You have done all your homework, have made the appointment, and have come to your appointment on time. As you meet a new customer, remember that the first impression is a lasting one. If you make a favorable first impression, it will help you considerably toward making the sale.

When you greet your prospect, do it cheerfully, with a smile and a handshake. Say, "Good morning," "Good evening," or "Good afternoon." Don't go in drooping, sad, or sulking; be cheery. Put your customers in a good mood such that they will be relaxed and happy. Remember, they are buying something; they're going to put their money out to purchase something. At least make them happy when they do it.

When you go into the customer's office, place your hat and coat on a chair next to you or in an outer office, if he doesn't suggest a place. Sit yourself where he suggests; if he doesn't suggest a particular spot for you to sit, adjust the setting to suit your needs. When in the home speaking with both he and his wife, arrange them in a position which would be more conducive to your demonstration. If you're in his office, then the chances are he will have designated a place for you to sit. And sit without slouching.

Don't smoke when you're trying to talk. If you smoke, look at yourself in the mirror sometimes and talk to yourself with a cigarette in your mouth; not only is it difficult to understand what you're saying, but it looks quite bad. It's extremely unprofessional.

Don't, in deference to your prospect, be overly gracious or patronizing. Don't revere him. Just show a certain amount of deference and a certain amount of graciousness, enough to satisfy his ego and to stamp you as a gentleman and as a professional.

Try not to become overly familiar with him. If you become familiar with your prospect, he may laugh, joke, and pat you on your back all the way out of his office, without a sale. Retain a small degree of aloofness. Retain a barrier between the two of you. Be warm, be sincere, be frank, but don't be overly friendly. Address him as "Mr. Smith"; don't call him by his first name unless he suggests it, and even then, unless he insists, use his title or surname.

The voice you use is also very important in your demonstration. Don't shout. Don't over punctuate your remarks; don't speak in a dull tone. Change your voice; modulate it to give emphasis to important points. Don't slur; talk very clearly. Don't talk too fast. Don't garble or swallow your words. Enunciate and pronounce each word distinctly. In a close space, if you're overly loud, you could possibly destroy the mood or confidence; your prospect may react harshly and develop a bitter mood toward you. Be firm, be in control, and command attention. Win respect, induce confidence, and make sure that he believes in you. Induce this believability. Remember that your voice is an extension of you and your personality. It's the most essential tool that you have. Develop and train it. Make it serve you. Make it aid you and use it to maximum effectiveness.

Further, the language that you use (words, phrases, sentences, even proper diction) is very important. What you say and how you say it reveal the kind of person you are as well as mirror your attitude, your character, and your personality. Your language should reflect the kind of person you are and should reflect your professionalism. It should also reflect the quality of the firm that you represent. Your language should be on the level of the people you're speaking to. Make sure they understand you.   D o n ' t overly impress people with long words when simple ones would be just as clear. Make sure, by all means, that you're understood.

Use colloquial expressions when they're needed to make a point, but avoid vulgar or slang words; don't use profanity or cuss words. They don't add anything to the clarity of your proposition and, in fact, detract greatly from the image that you're trying to convey. Avoid using long sentences, which usually hide or confuse the point that you're trying to make. Select your words very carefully. Use words that will add luster to your proposition. Remember that the words you are speaking have a definite meaning to your prospects. Try to perceive the impact you're making on them; weigh your words very carefully as to how your prospects will interpret them. Perceive their reaction to what you're saying. Make sure you're understood.

Avoid overworked, trite expressions that people use but are actually empty words. Words like "greatest," "best," "tremendous," "fantastic." Everybody uses these words so much that they have become meaningless. They are empty.

Also, avoid expressions or phrases that might create the opposite meaning from what you're trying to convey. People often use the expression "to be perfectly honest"; your customers expect you to be perfectly honest throughout your entire presentation. Why all of a sudden, they may think, would you become perfectly honest? And if now you're perfectly honest, what had you been before?   More examples are "to be frank with you," "as a matter of fact," "to show my sincerity." These are empty expressions. Buyers expect you to be honest and frank, to be factual and truthful and sincere with them. When you keep repeating these phrases, they may suspect that you're not as honest as you should be. Perhaps you're tending to distort the truth or exaggerate the facts.

In summary, the language that you use should be carefully thought out. It should be carefully and strategically planned. Keep in mind that the words you use have a meaning and will make an impression on listeners. Try to perceive the impression you are making on them. Make sure that you are saying what you want to say. Make sure they understand you. If they don't, if your prospects fail to understand you, the fault does not lie with them but with you. It's your obligation; in fact, it's your job to make yourself understood completely, without any ambiguity, without any general expressions, with specificity and to the point.

Showmanship

Showmanship uses imagination to create mental images of things that are not before him. In communicating, imagination is the ability to see an idea or article in use and to visualize new functions for it, and new ways to combine it with other ideas and/or products.

Avoid the use of "I," or "myself," or "me," unless it's absolutely necessary. Put yourself on the same level as the company; you're an extension of the company or product that you represent. It's "our" product. By so doing, you are connecting yourself with a prestigious product or company; you're trying to associate yourself with your product. In so doing, you try to raise your level by drawing on the value that the customer has for your product. Make language your servant. Make it your slave. Make it work for you. It'll be a willing servant if you're a benevolent master.

When you're presenting your proposition, let your enthusiasm work for you. This should not take the form of a loud-voiced argument but should be generated by confidence and genuine sincerity. It should smooth your progress toward your ultimate goal, which is to make the sale. A presentation without enthusiasm is like a birthday cake without candles. Show a sincere enthusiasm, an enthusiasm that comes from the knowledge that your product is the best and that you're doing something beneficial for your customer.

Feel connected with your prospects; put yourself in their position. Look from their point of view. See how it is from their side of the world. Identify yourself with them, with their emotions, hopes, and wants. As you get to understand them, you'll have a better idea of the impact that your proposition is making. It'll enable you to make your prospects the center of your presentation. Customer should constantly be focused in the main light of what you're trying to say. They are the center of attention.

Remember, you're trying to bring customers, very gently, in an orderly, step-by-step fashion, from their first degree of awareness of the proposition that you're presenting them with to the point where they want to buy your product; where they want to accept proposition.

Sometimes, showmanship involves doing something dramatic or unusual to create attention or capture interest. When I sold Kirby vacuum cleaners, one thing that I would do is throw dirt onto the carpet to demonstrate how strong the suction was and how thorough the cleaning would be. Another example was to vacuum the mattress and show the results. But, be careful. The mattress demonstration could embarrass the owner to the point that they may terminate the presentation.

Hence, how can the need for showmanship be overemphasized? It not only dramatizes the benefits that you indicate will accrue to buyers when they accept your proposal, it also emphasizes how they will appeal to all the senses; it doubles the impact. Showmanship is achievable in many ways through actually demonstrating the product, putting the product in the hands of your prospects so they can see it, feel it, operate it, and use it. Use visual aids, photographs, flip charts, diagrams, videos, pictures, or portfolios. Visual aids serve to clarify or illustrate the important points. They are very important. Use them, with a caveat.

Visual aids are excellent tools when they fit a situation, but they can be harmful distractions when they don't. If they are not specifically germane to the salient points being discussed, don't use them; they're not needed. If your company provides visual aids, they have been thoroughly researched; they've been market-tested, so make full use of them. You should plan the points in your presentation when these aids should be introduced, thus adding sparkle and showmanship to your sales story.

In pointing out a specific characteristic of your product, don't merely point it out; explain why it's important. If you're selling an automobile, and you say, "This motor has a 340-cubic-inch displacement," that's fine. But then explain why this fact is important for your prospect. Don't just say it; prove it. Don't be embarrassed by having the prospect, at a later point, ask, "Well, how do I know this is really so?" or "What good would that do me?" or "How do I know that this idea will work?" Voluntarily and deliberately, corroborate what you're saying by evidence and supporting affirmation during your presentation. Attempt to eliminate objections before they come up. Answer any questions before they come up in the course of your presentation.

Ways of doing this include citing anecdotal stories, success stories, cases that are similar to the ones you're suggesting now. Try to use other companies that your prospect knows about (without disclosing any trade secrets, as that could cost you not just one but two customers). Another type of corroboration is a signed testimonial letter from a satisfied customer who is using your product now. Bring out only those testimonials relevant to your particular situation. Don't bring out a portfolio with 150,000 different letters. Bring out the ones that are most applicable to the present situation.

This brings to mind one specific event that occurred in New Orleans. I started working for *Encyclopedia Britannica* in 1965, just after Hurricane Betsy hit New Orleans. It completely obliterated three-quarters of the lower lying areas in the New Orleans metropolitan area. One of the features that Britannica had at the time was an automatic insurance policy against fire or flood damage within a three-year period from the date of original purchase. During the course of a presentation, I learned that the customer was afraid of losing their set in another hurricane, as the levees still hadn't been rebuilt; she wanted to wait until later to buy. Aware of this, I proceeded to tell them about Britannica's insurance policy. There was still a degree of skepticism, until I had the customer call someone whose set we just replaced. When she learned that this policy was legitimate, and the set was actually replaced quickly, without any red tape, I closed my sale.

Don't be afraid to use live, on-the-spot testimony. Use it sparingly, but it can often affect the outcome of your presentation. It shows that you don't have anything to fear, that your company's policies can be checked on. Your proposition becomes more believable and more acceptable. Don't just say it; prove it.

To a considerable extent, competition may be anticipated and forestalled during the presentation. That is, salespeople should think about competition before facing the prospect, rather than waiting until the interview starts. They can meet the claims they know will be made, show the superiority of their product in those aspects. By so doing, they can shrink those competitive claims in the mind of the prospect before they are brought out into the open. This can be done without mentioning the competitor by name, thereby avoiding an argument or engaging in a rough knocking session.

It goes without saying that a thorough knowledge of competing products may underlie any such effort to eliminate them. This knowledge should include such matters as sales trends, performance, value of their dealers, advertising, sales promotion programs, various trade practices, and their real price. It is helpful to know just where your competition is vulnerable. Talk with owners of competing products. Be familiar with the claims made by your competitors. Watch their advertising, get ahold of their sales literature, and visit their showrooms, if you can. Ask your customers what they hear about competitors. Learn what competitors are saying about your product. Get a competitor to try to sell you, if possible. Finally, it would help if you can identify just where your chief competition lies in each particular sale so that you can slant your demonstration accordingly.

An attitude of absolute fairness toward competitors, even when it is necessary to speak disparagingly of their goods, should be encouraged. You should say nothing derogatory that cannot be substantiated at once, and you should be very careful about saying even that if it does not seem necessary. You will do well to avoid mentioning your competitors as much as possible. If comparisons are made, they should be made in a spirit of fairness. No statement should ever be made that cannot be backed up. The ethics of business are improving, and the salesperson must lead the way.

Paralleling the importance of speech is the necessity for the salesperson to listen to the customer. Many salespeople believe that sales can be made strictly by talking without listening. They're convinced that if they could just complete their presentation, the prospect would logically buy. Yet it doesn't happen like that. Salespeople can and do over talk to their detriment. You must learn when to stop talking; when to shut up; and when to listen. Listening is an indispensable quality of a professional salesperson.

Listening doesn't mean just not talking; listening means taking an active interest in what buyers have to say. Don't interrupt them, thinking that their words are a nuisance. Listen constructively to what they say. By listening and filling in between the lines, you can tell how prospect really feel. You can tell the impact, the effect that you're making on them with your presentation. And you can also tell how they really think.

Listening requires complete attention. It's necessary to concentrate your efforts and be responsive and sensitive to what the customer says. There are several important reasons for listening to customers actively and concentrating on what they say. Primary among them is the fact that prospects need to be listened to. They want someone to talk to, so listen to what they say. When you do so, they feel important and believe they have an active part in what is going on. It also gives them a feeling of respect that you took the time to listen to what they had to say.

Listening to customers will provide the necessary feedback on how the points of your presentation are affecting them. By listening to customers, you'll discover any hidden doubts or uncertainties that they have and hear the real objection they are making. But equally important, you give customers an opportunity to tell you why they want to buy your product or accepting your proposition. Listening to customers allows them to buy from you, rather than making you sell it to them. In most instances, reasons customers put forth in buying the product or accepting the proposition will aid you in subsequent sales.

How do we learn more? By listening. Most people are poor listeners. Basically, the problem is caused by the fact that we think much faster than we talk. Thus, only the tightest thought control makes it possible to listen effectively. The tendency to digress, to deviate, to sidetrack, to go astray is quite natural.

Good listening requires the following four mental activities:

1. Categorizing what is being said in order to think ahead of the speaker, anticipate where the discussion is going, and draw conclusions from the words spoken.
2. Weighing the evidence used by the speaker to support the points he is making.
3. Periodically reviewing and mentally summarizing what has been said thus far.
4. Throughout the talk, listening between the lines in search of a meaning that is not necessarily put into spoken words but may be implied. Paying attention to nonverbal communication (facial expressions, gestures, tone, or voice) adds meaning to the spoken words.

As we get ready to proceed into persuasion, let's take a moment to think about the approach and presentation. The objective of the approach is to make a favorable impression so that we can secure the prospect's attention in order to make our presentation. This was set up by the preapproach. The information gleaned during this phase is now used to make the sale.

Everything that we have been doing up to now has the goal of gaining attention, creating interest, developing rapport, and defining or creating desire. These are important points to remember:

1. Look successful: neat, clean, and presentable
2. Have a pleasant personality
3. Create a good impression

To do so, we keep in mind our discussions on clothing, physical characteristics, voice and language, and mannerisms.

Persuasion in Selling

The presentation must be persuasive if the customer is to feel a compelling need to buy at this time.

The presentation, the means by which we effect persuasion, is the pathway to closing the sale. Keep in mind that persuasion does not occur at one magical moment. Persuasion is a continuous, progressive effort that is the backbone of the presentation.

As we have established, a need is the lack of something; a want is the way we satisfy that need. [For example: we are hungry- our need is food; our want is a steak- how we satisfy our hunger (as opposed to chicken, depending on what we are selling).] It is incumbent upon us to insure that the need we are creating or identifying can be met by the solution that we are providing. It is important to remain alert and aware during our presentation that we are having the desired effect of creating a want for our proposition. And if we are not, we have to be quick to alter/adapt our presentation.

The task of salespeople is to persuade prospects that their needs and wants can be realized through using their product. Salespeople must create a need or a want in order to make the sale; they must discover what those needs and wants are and discuss them openly during the course of their presentation.

People "buy" what we propose because of a need; real or perceived. This need is dependent on perceptions, attitudes, beliefs, or personality; each differing from one situation to another. There always exists a binary choice: buy or not buy. To be successful, we have to bring the prospect to a new awareness. This can create a great amount of dissonance. Persuasiveness results when we bring about equilibrium.

The sales dynamic can be thought of in opposing scenarios: (A) the prospect knows that he has need but does not know how to satisfy it; or (B) the person does not know he has a need, and we make him aware of it. In either situation, the prospect has to be made aware of his problem (understand his need); be persuaded (convinced) that yours is the right solution; and be motivated to take action.

Persuasion involves appealing to the strongest instincts of prospects in an effort to secure their order and encourage them to buy at this time. And to appeal most effectively to these needs or wants, salespeople have the option of presenting the benefits from a desire for gain, fear of loss, or a combination of the two.

Persuasion involves motivation; the resulting aim is to induce action. When we persuade people to do something, we don't just change their way of thinking on the subject; we cause them to take action. Actions are modified as well as thoughts.

It is important that we keep our prospect psychologically "stable" through this process. We do so by means of our presentation. We tailor our presentation to make sure that the prospect is moving towards a positive state of mind, not a negative one.

Our presentation has to be adapted to accommodate the prospect's mental style. Is he a logically driven person who has to be led through a logical sequence to the conclusion? Is he a people oriented person moved by personality? Or, is he an emotion oriented person moved by feelings, emotions, and taking action?

Some of the steps in this process we have already covered, such as knowing when to stop talking and when to listen; and using questions to our advantage. All of those steps make us aware of the problem and the solution, suggesting to us how to persuade and/or motivate the prospect to act in the manner we are suggesting.

Salespeople's efforts to persuade are based on an understanding of buying motives and on the facts that they have learned about their prospect; a sale will only be made when the prospects are persuaded that it is in their best interest to buy. Therefore, emphasis is placed on the interest of the prospect; salespeople must avoid calling attention to benefits they will receive.

As stated before, the fundamental aspects of persuasion are suggestion and logical reasoning (suggestion taking precedence). Humans are not essentially reasoning creature. In fact, most people scarcely reason at all. All of their actions are usually the result of imitation, habit, or suggestion. Psychologists will bear this out; most of our actions are only reactions. People accept as true every idea that enters their mind, unless a contradictory idea blocks this acceptance.

Additionally, most people will act according to idea that enter their mind, unless they cannot do so. This is the principle upon which modern-day advertising is based: statements that are repeated and not denied tend to be accepted. Salespeople use those principles during the presentation and close. They will fill out the order, thereby suggesting an act of writing. When they hand the prospect a pen with the suggestion, "Please sign this agreement where indicated," the prospect will generally go along with this idea.

Salespeople use different types of suggestions. Some of these suggestions are based on habit. Other suggestions are based on instincts, instincts that are fundamental and reliable, although habits may sometimes override them. The important point to bear in mind, from the standpoint of salesman, is to know when to use a suggestion. Obviously, suggestions cannot be used continuously, to the total exclusion of logical reason. A median has to be found, a balance between the use of logical reasoning and suggestion. Many effective suggestions are directed at subconscious motives, motives that have no rationale in them. In essence, a suggestion is simply a stimulus to imagination. When suggestions are strong enough, they hold prospects and hypnotize them into nothing but the suggestion. When salespeople use suggestions, they induce an imaginative experience on the part of the prospect.

Without doubt, people are easily suggestible, but their reaction depends on their desires, attitudes, ideas, and convictions. When salespeople make a careful preapproach, they are in a position to move their prospect into the action of buying. Suggestions are being used every day, by you and against you. The gas station attendant who walks up to you and asks, "May I fill it up, you'll get a free car wash?" is using a suggestion against you. Unless you are short on cash, you will generally go along with the idea of filling your gas tank. When you stop by a friend's office and suggest, "You need a cup of coffee; I'm treating," then that friend will undoubtedly go along with the suggestion (unless he has something that prevents him from going). Therefore, it is important to realize the value of suggestion and the ways in which suggestions can be used and employed, both for you and against you.

Close and Departure

Now, we are ready for the climax of all of our efforts: the close! Everything heretofore is directed to this one moment: knowing when the buyer is ready to buy! It is then our responsibility to **help** our prospect acquire the satisfaction to the need we have just identified and/or created. We never ask, we always assume, and then we lead to the acquisition.

Although I am devoting a separate chapter to the close, let me emphasize that it is also an integral part of the presentation. The close is not something apart, but rather the single most important part of the presentation. The close results from a series of agreements, either stated or implied, that have taken place during the presentation. The close is formed step-by-step, point by informational point, through suggestions, questions, and arousing interest as you make prospects realize that it is indeed important for them to have your product or proposition.

The close is the culmination of all your efforts up to this point. If you can't close, you can't sell. A football team can pile up five hundred yards in offense, but if it doesn't score any points, none of that offense does any good. The opponent may have only have one yard of offense, but if in that yard, it managed to cross the goal line, it wins the game. Winning the game means making the sale. And the key to making the sale lies in your close.

The close does not consist of one magical moment when the customer is ready to buy. Rather, the close is a series of steps that culminate in the customer's signing the agreement. These steps should be taking place during your entire presentation.

Good salespeople know more than just one close; they know ten or fifteen of them. And they don't just use two or three closes; they use four, five, or six closes during the course of their presentation and sale.

The close amounts to a summary of the presentation and a completion of the transaction by consummating the sale. Now by this, I don't mean that you ask the customer, "Are you ready to make the deal now?" or "Okay, let's buy." You're not going to say, "Here, take the pen; now sign," or "What's your decision?" Rather, through suggestion, you bring buyers to the point where they are willing to buy.

If you come right out and say "Okay, now buy," even if they were ready to buy, they might refuse. What is necessary for a good close is a summary of the logical reasons and benefits presented to customers, indicating why they should buy your product.

Assume the Sale

Then, assume the sale. You must automatically assume that the presentation was such that your prospects will know how important it is for them to have this product; they will realize the benefits accruing to them through your product and thus buy it.

Bear in mind that today, buyers want help from salespeople, based on their knowledge of the product and of the customer's needs. Customers welcome assistance from salespeople in making decisions easier. They want the salesperson to help them buy what's right for them, and this is precisely what the summary is all about. If the presentation was logical, intelligible, comprehensible, and specific, and if it pointed out how the product would bring them certain benefits, then they will buy. You have removed the indecision from the buying process. You have shown the prospects that it is in their best interests to make the decision to buy.

You are making the presentation in order to make a sale. Your prospect knows that you're trying to make a sale; don't shy around it, disguise it, or conceal the fact. During your summary, bring out your order form and write details on the back of it: prices, shipping dates, a breakdown of the monthly payments, color choices. Bringing out the order form makes it seem natural to prospects to have the order form in front of them. By bringing out the order form, it is a simple step to turning it over and writing up the order.

This is the assumptive close. You have assumed that they are ready to buy. You bring out the order form or agreement. Never call it a contract; always call it "an agreement" or "the deal." As you prepare to have them sign the agreement, never say, "Sign here." Say, "Would you please okay this agreement?" indicating where they are supposed to sign.

As you start writing the agreement, ask customers questions, such as which color they want, if they've decided on thirty monthly payments or ninety days without interest, or when they want delivery. When customers see you writing up the agreement, they are faced with the decision. You have in effect silently suggested that they are going to buy.

Now if they are not ready to buy, they will protest at this point. They may say, "Well, I haven't decided whether or not I am really going to buy," or they will answer the questions you're putting to them, in which case, you've made the sale. If they hesitate or do not sign the agreement, then you have to start selling again until they are ready for another close.

These are important points of the close to remember:

1. Bring customers to the buying point.
2. The moment you feel they are ready, try to take their order.
3. Don't ask directly to buy; without giving offense, take for granted that the customers are going to buy and set up details as though they've said yes.
4. If customers are not ready to buy, drop the order book and start selling again.

Objection Control

Related to presentations and closing is the subject of how to overcome objections. Invariably during the course of the presentation, unless customers are already willing to buy your product, they will raise some questions or present reasons for not buying. This is called an objection.

The most disastrous mistake you can make is to react insulted or annoyed when customers raise objections.

Objections should not be viewed as interruptions to your presentation or roadblocks to the progress of the sale. That would be a misunderstanding of what the customer is actually doing. Listening to objections is an important way to monitor the impression that you're making on the customer or the success you're having making the sale.

A professional salesperson should be sensitive to objections and should be aware of their true meaning and significance. And although some objections might seem petty, or invalid, they are actually beneficial to the sale. Objections, instead of being roadblocks, are actually signs indicating the progress that you're making toward your final goal, which is making the sale. Many times, when customers present an objection, it really means that they want more information. Perhaps you haven't made yourself completely clear, or perhaps one of your selling points is ambiguous. Customers will want this point clarified, and you can do this by giving them more information.

Another reason for an objection is when customers want reassurance. Your prospects may be sold on the idea; they may be ready to buy, but want to be reassured that they are making the right decision. They want to be certain that the facts you presented them justify their decision to buy your product or prposal.

Prospects may accept every point in your story but one, and their objection is on this one point only. They bring it up, and it's a valid objection. If you clear up this point, then the sale is made. Equally as important, though, customers prove by asking questions that you definitely have their attention and they are interested. They are paying close attention to what you're saying.

The type of question, and the point at which this question comes up, is a key to the progress that you're making (in real time) during your presentation. It's an indication that you may not be getting through to them. What you need to do at this point is to stop and go over the vital points of your presentation, the reasons that you covered for them to buy your product.

Ideally, you try to anticipate the objections that your prospects will come up with. This is done by researching the typical objections that are raised concerning your product. This is done through meetings and conversations with other salespeople and by past experience with other customers. However, this is only ideally.

More often than not, your presentation may omit certain facts, fail to clarify a point, or raise some doubts. These objections will be raised, and the extent to which you're able to cope with them will determine the outcome of your presentation. It will determine whether you make a sale or not. When an objection comes up, relax, stay calm, and welcome the fact that the customer has made an objection. Smile and say, "That's a very good point; I'm glad you brought it up," or "That's a logical question; it shows that we're thinking along the same lines," or "I failed to mention one point; let me bring it up now."

Listen to the objections that prospects make. Listen to it very attentively. Don't interrupt them. Let them talk. Hear what they are saying. Read between the lines for significant voice intonations, inflexions, or special emphasis.

In order to demonstrate to prospects that you have been listening to them and you understand their objection, restate it in your own words. For example, ask, "Is this what you mean?" or "Is this really your question?" Then, very frankly, very calmly, with facts, with information, with proof, and with reassurance, respond to the objection and proceed with your presentation.

Sometimes, it's a good idea to restate your prospect's question or objections in the form of another question. For instance, if a prospect were to say, "I'm not going to buy the computer because my children can go to the library," an acute salesperson would respond, "What you want to know, Mr. Prospect, is why you should buy this computer when your children can use the one in the library; is that correct?"

The customer may respond, "Yes, that's exactly what I want to know."

Now the salesperson can point out the benefits and the reasons for the customer to have the product now. The salesperson will explain, show, and convince prospects that they will, in fact, profit from the product at this time.

Never ignore an objection a prospect raises. It's not only rude, but it's very bad strategy, as it may cause the customer to doubt that you know the answer. Don't disregard an objection, no matter how small it might seem, for although it might appear trivial to you, it could loom very large in the customer's mind. Second, minimize an objection. The worst thing that a salesperson can do is to have a confrontation with a prospect.

A salesperson should never say, "You're wrong about that," "That's not right," or "That's not true." Act glad that prospects wish to consider every side of a proposition; let them feel that the objection is natural from their point of view. Never enter a debate with prospects, and never flatly contradict them, as you may arouse their competitive spirit. Never suggest an objection for the purpose of refuting it.

No matter what happens, unless forcibly attacked, never argue with customers. Let customers talk as loudly or as nastily as they like; keep your temper. Discuss the matter quietly, and swallow your anger. Remember, the objective is to secure the order. You can relieve your frustration with the satisfaction of having made the sale.

Salespeople should try to find some part of the objection they can agree with and then turn it around and say, "Yes, Mr. Prospect, I can see where you have a valid point there," or "I tend to agree with you on this matter, but …" and then proceed with your rebuttal. Your rebuttal should consist of data, information, reassurance, or whatever else is required to quash the objection or answer the question.

Here are the most common types of objections that you will probably encounter, regardless of the product or proposition:

Price: "The price is too high." This will probably be the most difficult of all objections to overcome. The salesperson will hear it time and time again in just about every presentation made. Unfortunately, not every prospect can financially afford your product. In most cases, you're dealing with people who have to live within their budget.

There are a lot of quick comebacks that you can interject at this point, but being witty may not result in a sale. If the customer says your price is too high and then proceeds to explain why it's too high, then this is a legitimate, justifiable objection.

However, if price is something that's just mentioned capriciously, chances are it's a smoke screen covering up something else. You must get the customer to be more specific. If customers say, "Your price is too high", ask, "What makes you feel that it's too high?" or "Compared to what is it too high?" Make sure that they tell you why they feel the price is too high.

Depending on the basis for this objection, there are various ways to counter a claim that the price is too high. If the product is being compared to a competitive product at a lower price, make sure that the products are equivalent, with the same specifications and using the same materials. Perhaps the lower price involves a product with inferior raw materials or lower quality than your product. Make sure that the specifications are the same.

Another way to counter the price objection is to present the price in terms of an investment. Customers can buy another product for less money, but explain that they are making an investment, an investment into the future. Rather than have to pay now and then pay again in the future, they can make a onetime investment that will save money in the long term.

The point that needs be made is that your higher priced item is of a better quality; therefore, it will be less expensive in the long run. Point out the effect of buying a product of inferior quality, with poorer service, or from a less reliable firm. Besides, if the competing product sells at a cheaper price, it's probably because that company knows what its product is worth (this can be a very powerful comeback, if used effectively).

Also bear in mind that the price objection might be hiding a concern, deep feeling, or need for reassurance that the product is worth the price. Prospects sometimes use this ploy to get you to reduce your price.

People are willing to pay the price for quality, if that's what they want. Therefore, you must convince them that your product (although more expensive) is of a better quality than the others.

Remember, too, that smart buyers generally know what they're getting into; they're aware that they only get what they pay for and that higher prices are usually synonymous with higher quality. Emphasize that a cheaper object will probably be of lower quality than a higher priced item. Be frank and sincere with your prospect. By pointing out the benefit that can be accrued by buying your product as opposed to another one, you can succeed in making the sale.

Point out the benefits the customer will acquire by buying your product over a competitor's. After all, this is part of selling. By logically and systematically pointing out of the benefits, the quality, and the reasons that your product is better, you will make the sale.

Another frustrating objection is that the prospect intends to buy from a friend or a relative who sells a similar product. Now, if the friend sells an inferior product, you can overcome this by saying, "Mr. Prospect, I realize that your friend sells a similar product. I further realize that you want to help your friends as much as possible. And I further hope that maybe someday you will regard me as a friend also.

"However, a matter as important as this should be made on a stronger basis than merely friendship. In fact, sometimes, our friends tend to take us for granted and not give us the best deal, don't they?"

By using this type of approach, salespeople then proceed into their presentation and build up the points that are beneficial to their prospect buying their product or proposal. If these beneficial points have been presented properly, the prospect may realize they are really missing something by dealing with a friend.

Other objections that merit discussing are those along the following lines: "I am sorry, things are really bad right now; call me back at a later time," or "Things are really tight; I used up all my funds. I'll contact you later, when things are a little better," or "Business is really terrible." Those few examples will serve to illustrate some of the forms that those objections take. Although these objections are really a cover-up for other reasons, they are often difficult to discount.

The salesperson must show that there is never a better time to buy, since nothing generally changes. There is always something coming up. If things are bad today, they'll be bad next year; there's really never a better time. The best time to buy is now.

In order to show this, the salesperson could say, "Mr. Prospect, really and truly, there is no better time to buy than now. By waiting until later, you will be paying more for what you buy, and you will also be depriving yourself and your family of the benefits that can be derived from this product right now.

"Further, you and I both know that there will be no better time to buy than now. And if you wait, you probably will never have it. I am here now, you have seen the product, and you want and need the product, so now is the best time to buy."

Professional salespeople don't fear objections; they welcome them because objections reveal a prospect's thoughts and feelings. It represents a desire for more information. It indicates the rate of progress that your presentation is making. It also clarifies and removes obstacles to making the sale that could come up later.

Rather than being stumbling blocks and/or roadblocks, objections are signs that guide the customer toward acceptance of your product. By speaking with other salespeople, by drawing on past experiences, by the use of integrity and sensitivity, you can learn to overcome objections and clear the way toward a very successful selling career.

Buttoning up the Order

Once you've made the sale, your job is not over. After you've made the sale, after you've written the agreement, thank the buyer and express the feeling that he is now part of a team that is working to serve him. Express to the customer a feeling that now, more than ever, you would like his friendship and his cooperation. Remember, a salesperson's job is not just to sell the customer; it's also to keep him. It involves a long series of gestures that are intended not necessarily to cement the sale and button up the order, but also to make the customer a permanent asset. You can generate many more sales through this new customer's word-of-mouth advertising. Make him a member of your team. Make him help you through referrals and by being a satisfied proponent of your product.

A satisfied customer is the best advertisement that you could ever hope to obtain. It also avoids cancellations. The customer has to be reassured.

Leave him with a feeling that he has done the right thing; eliminate any chance for buyer's remorse; eliminate the opportunity for him to think he made a mistake with his purchase. Assure him; reassure him. This is called buttoning up an order.

Leaving Gracefully

And there I stood, with the order in my hand, muttering something about being grateful while the buyer just sat there, giving me a pained look. Finally, he said, "All you have to do, son, is turn around and walk out the door; it's as easy as that." I was so embarrassed. "Nobody ever told me what to do after I got the order," a new representative for an abrasive manufacturer said painfully. It had not occurred to him that a graceful departure is an important part of the selling process.

But think one moment; a good departure sets the stage for the next approach to that prospect. Wise salespeople leave with their fences mended and bridges intact.

When the salesperson is ready to leave, one of two things has happened: the sale has either been made or not.

Sale Made

First, let us assume that the sale has been made. In this case, you must guard against certain dangerous faults. If you're inexperienced, you may be reacting to the nervous tension you've been under. In this reaction, your prime feeling is one of thankfulness that the interview is over and the order attained. Under an impulse of gratitude and relief, it is easy to grow effusive in thanking customers for their order. There is a tendency to release the pent-up emotion in a flood of talk (bordering on the semi hysterical if you're inexperienced). Here is the place to keep a tight rein on your feelings and a close watch on your emotions and actions.

Remember that the sale is a mutually profitable transaction; buyers have neither done you a favor nor received one. They will have less respect for you and less confidence in the product if you reveal by your attitude that getting an order is a rare event. You should thank the buyer for the order but not overly effusively. You should act as if this was a natural and expected occurrence.

You should turn the conversation into other channels, perhaps regarding a new advertising campaign, a successful method practiced by other purchasers, or any matter of general interest to the buyer.

While the prospect is signing, you should not stage a dramatic silence; instead, maintain a conversation. This is very important. Maintain an unhurried, friendly conversation, as if the act of getting an order was a commonplace affair. As you gather up your possessions and prepare to take your leave, you may remark, "Thank you for your courtesy and for the order. I'll be on my way to get things moving on it properly," or "You've made a very wise choice, Mr. Prospect. Goodbye and thank you." Another possible statement to take leave would be "Congratulations and welcome to our product family."

This raises the question as to whether you should depart at once or linger for a time. And, of course, this depends on certain factors. But it is safe to say that you should always be the first to rise. The most important factor is whether or not the buyer wants you to stay. Sometimes, if the buyer wants to chitchat a bit, the time may be right for a friendly conversation together. However, I recommend not smoking while with customers.

Perhaps the prospect is social and offers you a cup of coffee or a drink. Some people may become offended if refused. Feel the situation out; take the pulse of the atmosphere. Diagnose the sincerity of their offer, and if you feel that it's genuinely sincere, then go ahead and be social with the prospect.

Those who advocate a quick departure to avoid having buyers change their mind or cancel their order lack an understanding of the principles of what has just occurred.

If the sale has been made thoroughly, there is little danger of buyers changing their minds at the last minute. But if they are going to change their minds, in all probability, it will occur whether you linger or depart in a hurry. Prospects who are fully convinced of the value of your product will not consider losing this benefit. If they are not so convinced, they may cancel the order after you leave, anyway. It's an indication of weak salesmanship if you fear such hidden cancellations.

A second blunder that you can commit after successfully completing the sale is to assume a superior attitude, as though feeling you've won a victory. You may emit an air of condescension that would insult your customer and result in cancellation and certainly in the loss of future business. The fact that customers have bought the product does not remove them from the list of prospective purchasers for the future. Now is the time to start the next sale, to leave with a feeling of satisfaction that will bring them back. This is the preapproach to the next sale. The departure then is merely the beginning of a follow-up.

Sale Not Made

The departure when a sale has not been made should be very similar as to that when the sale is made, with a few basic changes. To begin with, your attitude when you've lost a sale should be no different from that of a successful salesperson. Of course, this is easier said than done. It takes a good sport to smile and act friendly after failing to make a hard prospect see the light, but it must be done.

After an unsuccessful call on a prospect, a salesman called a second time. After putting his signature on a liberal order, the buyer burst out, "Say, young fellow, do you know you're the first salesman who ever went away without an order who actually thanked me for the time I gave him? You sold me these goods when you were here before."

If an interview results in no sale, you must avoid these three responses: scorn, anger, and inferiority. If you're a real artist, you will be able to sense the certain turndown before it arrives and contrive to make an unpretentious getaway. You will deftly guide the conversation into new channels, without a break, finally rising and perhaps remarking, "Well, I've got to be getting on. I've enjoyed our visit and will look in again sometime soon. Goodbye."

The purpose of making such a getaway is to leave the door open for a return. You've prevented the prospect from turning you down flatly and finally.

The prospect has not definitely gone on record as being opposed to the proposition or product, so there's a better chance to reopen the sale.

However, a grave danger connected with this method should be mentioned. If you use it too often, you may acquire the callback habit. The idea should be instilled in your mind that you try hard to sell at the first interview.

Some sales managers have gone a little further and said that you should never do callbacks. Those managers feel that if you burn your bridges behind you, you will be more apt to fight vigorously for an immediate sale. But where the interview is being conducted under serious difficulties, making it suicidal to attempt a close, the next best thing is to effect a graceful exit, leaving the door open for another interview later, with possible sale.

It has often been said that sales, as with all of life, is a game of percentages. No one is going to win all the time. The more presentations you make, the more opportunity there is to win and make a sale. Thus, leaving the door open for a later approach increases the opportunity to maximize your time and make a sale. Keep in mind that you've already invested considerable time and effort in each prospect.

Reasons for not buying on the first call may include the fact that customers really cannot afford it. And if they honestly do not have the money, you cannot fault them for that. Other reasons are that they don't have the authority to buy without approval. Maybe you have presented the proposition to someone who needs approval from a spouse (in the case of a personal purchase), a superior, a committee, or a board of directors. Perhaps company policy requires additional bids or information on other competing products.

Maybe the customer wants to study the facts and figures. Or maybe they really do not make decisions on the spur of the moment. They may want to work it out and then decide after consulting with others or weighing the benefits.

In most cases, this means that you have lost the sale. But remember, if you've tried everything possible and still don't make the sale, leave the door open for future callbacks. Thank them sincerely for the courtesy they extended to you in listening to your presentation. Accept the fact that they are not going to buy. Don't act disappointed, pout, or imply that your prospect is stupid for not buying; don't force the issue. Don't make a nuisance out of yourself. Don't lose your temper or try to browbeat your prospect into buying. In short, don't act like a sore loser. You're a professional. Uphold your image as a professional, and it will go a long way in making future sales.

Part V

Motivation

Success is a state of mind, a pattern, and a way of living, of doing a lot of little things well, every day. Contrary to mistaken belief, motivation is not the sole basis for success; you must have ability, training, and knowledge to achieve specific goals.   Thus, the difference between success and failure in everything you do is determined by how much ability and motivation you possess. The two are not synonymous.

At this point, if you have read and absorbed everything written thus far, you should be able to sell any product in the world, any place in the world, to any person under the sun.

Now, we will strive to motivate you to use those newly acquired talents, your new ability, in a way that is most beneficial and that grants you the best chance for success. Motivation is just as important in selling as the approach, presentation, and close.

The ability to motivate yourself, the ability to use the knowledge and training you have to the fullest, will positively govern the results you gain from life. Motivation has made many individuals great. It has captured human minds since the beginning of time. And is the single most determining factor in winning, selling, and being successful.

So what is motivation? How do you achieve motivation? And how do you motivate yourself? While no one can answer those questions for you, we can give insight and understanding into what motivation is and how it works. If you have the desire and are willing to make drastic changes in your habits and thinking, you can determine what motivating forces are at work within yourself and direct those forces toward enriching your life and fulfilling your goals, desires, and ambitions.

What is the difference between the Super Bowl Champion and the loser? What made Joe Montana, Miss America, The President of the United States, or Marilyn Monroe so special?

Each of them possessed different physical characteristics, mental abilities, environmental conditioning, personality, grooming, ambition, work habits, training habits, diet, education, and interests.

People behave in many unexpected, and sometimes uncharacteristic, ways. We often refer to these differences as multidimensional. No one is exactly alike. Nevertheless, certain general characteristics can be observed to be similar, if not actually the same; certain patterns begin to appear.

The one important factor that emerges as the principle reason for their success is the fact people differ in their reasons for doing things. People satisfy their needs in different ways. And getting people to understand what their reasons for doing things are, and how to activate those reasons, is the essence of motivation.

By understanding basic principles of what drives a person to action, what motivates that person, you can not only determine and direct your own behavior but the customer's as well.

I heard the following story long ago but forgot who told it to me. I have recalled it all these years because it brings home the importance of being motivated and not being influenced by negative factors.

The Empty Office

A successful executive in a large company went on vacation. During this vacation, the company president, as a reflection of the respect and appreciation he had for this trusted employee, ordered his office redecorated and refurnished with fine new furniture. The president had hoped this would be a pleasant surprise, but the job took longer than expected.

The vacationing executive returned to his office early on the Monday morning that his vacation was up. His office was bare of all furniture. Others had not yet come in. His immediate interpretation was, *I've been fired. I'm no longer wanted here.* He went home, emotionally shaken. He wrote a note to the president that he intended to mail to him. Fortunately, he tore it up. He couldn't figure out why the president had fired him.

By evening, he finally gathered courage. He felt that at least he deserved an explanation from the president and though others might ridicule him for fighting city hall, he would return the next morning to· ask for an explanation. He would not accept termination without a fight. When he arrived next morning, the president met him in the hall, welcomed him back, told how he was missed, and apologized for not having the finer quarters completed.

What happened? Instead of believing in himself and taking the time to understand what was going on, the executive took the easy way out. He simply believed that he was not going to succeed, not going to make the sale, not going to win, and was willing to walk away from his entire life. The same person responsible for taking action is responsible for the interpretations others may make of that action (and these interpretations often affect the feelings of customers). Finally, only when he became sufficiently motivated based on his desire to keep his job, did he rely on his confidence and fight for his job.

What Is Motivation?

There is one principle that needs to be emphasized, and reemphasized, and that is that no matter how much you learn, no matter how good you become, YOU WILL NOT MAKE EVERY SALE! YOU WILL NOT ALWAYS ACCOMPLISH YOUR GOAL! And YOU WILL NOT SOLVE ALL PROBLEMS!

President Roosevelt, the only person to win 4 terms as president of the United States (before the term limit amendment was passed), at his inauguration, stated: "The greatest fear we face is fear itself".

And that is even truer for anyone who aspires to be a salesperson, aspires to communicate to another, or who aspires to achieve their goals. In other words, for all of us!

Most people do not fear selling per say; they do not fear making a presentation, meeting objections, or closing. They fear being told NO!

Why? Because it makes them feel diminished, belittled, rejected, and ignored. It makes them feel like a failure; it makes them feel less confident. And to a salesperson, confidence is the single most important trait that he must develop and possess.

But, the fact is, being told no is not a personal failure or attack against you. It is part of the process in any interaction between people. Being told no is part of being engaged in The People Business. Unfortunately, no matter how good your proposition is, no matter how needed you service, product, idea, or innovation is, there are some that will not "buy" into it.

You will not make every sale, and you will not always get a chance to make a presentation. This does not reflect on your skills, abilities, or personality. It is simply the nature of the business, the nature of the people business! This is normal and expected.

When it happens, when you are told no, embrace it knowing that you have just moved closer to a sale. Selling is a numbers game subject to percentages and the law of averages. The average now favors you.

Fear of failure is debilitating. It causes us to freeze and not move forward. It prevents us from solving problems. It prevents us from achieving our goals.

Fear of rejection keeps the beauty queen at home on date nights, the pretty girl at home on prom nights. Fear of being told no prevents us from trying. You can't win the lottery if you don't buy a ticket. You can't succeed if you don't risk failure; you can't be told yes if you don't risk being told no.

If we don't risk failure, if we don't risk being told no, we can never experience success!

Sometimes we will make mistakes and those mistakes will lead to being told no. Sometimes, we will not make the right decisions and this will result in our "failure". But as my Father of blessed memory taught me: "It is not what a person does that determines his true character; but it is how one reacts to what he does that determines his character.

Anyone can err; but not just anyone can admit what has been done, learn from it, and overcome this error to achieve success. And, what character trait must we possess to enable to overcome being told no? Confidence!

Don't think that you have to have an original thought; but realize that your thoughts are an amalgamation of all of your experiences; it is a fusion of all you have learned (good, and yes, bad) from all of the people you have met, spoken to, listened to, heard from, or read about. Be confident that you have processed and honed all of your skills to maximize your abilities. And, this confidence, arrogance if you will, will keep you strong and ready for the next opportunity.

Remember, the key to success in sales, in communicating, is to place yourself in a position to make your presentation. That is all you want, that is the most you can ask for. For the more presentations you make, the more you tell your story, the more you risk being told no to, the more you will succeed. The more you will sell.

Motivation is the term I use to explain why people behave like they do. Motivation is that which causes behavior, whatever incites action. Motivation is not the action itself, but the catalyst propelling that action.

What this definition effectively implies would seem to be the mainspring of success: the characteristics that drive one person to achieve a particular end that another individual with similar endowments apparently lacks.

Motivation is ordinarily indicated by such words as *want, wish,* and *desire,* and it's commonly contrasted with ability. For example, although you may be able to play tennis, you may not want to play. In other words, you are not motivated to play. And if you were to play in that state, you could easily lose to a player with less ability.

What quality distinguishes people who are successful from those of equal ability, mentality, background, and training who fail? What gives some people energy and drive, while others are listless and drifting? Why do some people lead lives of satisfaction and accomplishment, while others continually face frustration and despair?

The answer lies in one magical, mystical quality: motivation. We have seen this quality at work many times throughout history where supposedly weaker people of lesser ability triumphed over vastly superior opponents.

We saw the power of motivation at work when little David slew Goliath and when Samson beat the Philistines. We saw it more recently when a very small state, forged out of the wilderness, motivated by the will to succeed and the desire for survival, fought not only an army but three nations simultaneously and emerged victorious. Of course, I am referring to the State of Israel.

How often do we see a fighter climb into the ring, supposedly with no chance whatsoever of winning, and score a knockout in the first round? What is the quality that enables a weaker team to rise to the occasion and thoroughly beat a stronger, more able team?

Very simply stated, one side was motivated, while the other was not. Regarding this, we often hear people say, "They wanted it more." There are many kids with as much stamina, muscle, and talent as gold medal winners, yet they lack the motivation to be great; they simply did not want it as much.

Motivation, then, is that invaluable, invisible ingredient that propels people to action, full of drive, energy, and purpose. Motivation is a guiding light that illuminates the path leading to success and happiness.

How to Motivate Yourself and Others

The single most important ingredient for success is the ability to motivate others or yourself.

Too often, we attempt to motivate people and ourselves by blindly following an assumption that's untrue; that is, we think we must motivate by appealing to what they want: money, recognition, or other material benefits.

Yet motivation as a great power is not wanting; it is believing. Believing in what you are doing and that you can actually accomplish your objectives, regardless of the perceived (real or imaginary) obstacles. All things are possible to those who believe. Motivation, then, is something people develop for themselves. It does not come from the outside in, but rather from the inside out. As Bob Conklin says, "Deep motivation does not develop from wanting, circumstances, people, or a job, but it is grown in the heart and mind of the individual through the power of belief."

And belief begins with knowledge. The more knowledge you have about something, the more interest you have, and the more you want to learn. You must have an interest before you have belief. How can you believe in something you know nothing about?

Continuing, how can you be motivated about something you know little about or find bewildering? The answer is simple: you can't. You must find the time for further learning and instruction. Never feel that you know enough.

It is ironic, perhaps, that the more you know about something, the more you realize that you really have a lot more to learn. Stop learning, and you stop believing. You must continue to learn, to gain knowledge about your job, company, or product in order to maintain interest, which leads to belief, which in turn leads to motivation.

Equally as important, belief is the realization and conviction that you are acting, working, and using your life for a worthwhile purpose, that your efforts are productive and useful. It is impossible to believe in any principle, subject, or activity that your conscience will not accept.

Thus, your belief must not compromise your honesty or ethics. The activity you believe in must be based on honesty, sincerity, and trust.

You must have faith and confidence that your company's product fulfills its stated claims. But further, you must be truly convinced that yours is a needed job, in a needed place. Do not allow yourself to be caught in negative thoughts, that your job is not important or success will never be yours. Otherwise, you will find yourself simply going through the motions, with minimal effort and no enthusiasm. This is a certain recipe for failure. Your job is important if you believe it is.

Remember, if your job was unimportant, it would not exist, and you would not be there. Everything is part of a team effort; every job is an integral and important part of the whole.

The salesperson's job is just as important as the manufacturer's or producer's, if not more. Even the machinist who produces the product is just as important as, if not more than, the president of the company. There is no company without a product, and all of the products in the world are meaningless and worthless without salespeople to bring them to market.

If you believe that your job is important, then you will be motivated to do the best possible job, and you will motivate others. And this motivation, more than any other single quality, will bring you success, happiness, and satisfaction.

References

Irving Allen

Irving Allen was a theatrical and cinematic producer and director. He won an Academy Award in 1948 for producing the short movie Climbing the Matterhorn. In the early 1950s he formed Warwick Films with partner Albert "Cubby" Broccoli and relocated to England to leverage film making against a subsidy offered by the British government. Through the 1950s they each became known as one of the best independent film producers of the day, as the two would sometimes work in tandem, but more often than not on independent projects for their joint enterprise producing multiple projects in a given year.

Arthur H. Motley

Arthur H. Motley, a onetime Fuller brush salesman who became president and publisher of the fledgling Parade Magazine and turned it into one of the most profitable Sunday supplements in newspaper history retired in 1978, lived 83.

"He's the greatest salesman God ever created," one of his colleagues said in 1959. Mr. Motley was an outspoken man who was once described as having a thatch of flaming red hair and a foghorn voice. His hair provided him with the nickname "Red" that he loved to scrawl in red crayon at the bottom of notes to Parade's writers.

Charles Newbold

Charles Newbold was an American blacksmith born in 1780 in Chesterfield Township, New Jersey. On June 26, 1797, Newbold received the first patent for a cast-iron plow. However, he was unable to sell his plow because many farmers feared that the iron in it would poison the soil.

King C. Gillette

King Camp Gillette was an American businessman. He invented a bestselling version of the safety razor. Several models were in existence before Gillette's design. Gillette's innovation was the thin, inexpensive, disposable blade of stamped steel. Gillette is widely credited with inventing the so-called razor and blades business model, where razors are sold cheaply to increase the market for blades, but in fact he only adopted this model after his competitors did.

Thomas Edison

Thomas Alva Edison was an American inventor and businessman, who has been described as America's greatest inventor. He developed many devices that greatly influenced life around the world, including the phonograph, the motion picture camera, and the long-lasting, practical electric light bulb. Dubbed "The Wizard of Menlo Park", he was one of the first inventors to apply the principles of mass production and large-scale teamwork to the process of invention, and because of that, he is often credited with the creation of the first industrial research laboratory.

Elias Howe

Elias Howe Jr. was an American inventor and sewing machine pioneer. Elias Howe Jr. was born on July 9, 1819 to Dr. Elias Howe Sr. and Polly Howe in Spencer, Massachusetts. Howe spent his childhood and early adult years in Massachusetts where he apprenticed in a textile factory in Lowell beginning in 1835. After mill closings due to the Panic of 1837, he moved to Cambridge, Massachusetts, to work as a mechanic with carding machinery, apprenticing along with his cousin Nathaniel

Andrew Carnegie

Andrew Carnegie was a self-made steel tycoon and one of the wealthiest businessmen of 19th century. He later dedicated his life to philanthropic endeavors. He was born on November 25, 1835, in Dunfermline, Scotland. After moving to the United States, he worked a series of railroad jobs. By 1889 he owned Carnegie Steel Corporation, the largest of its kind in the world. In 1901 he sold his business and dedicated his time to expanding his philanthropic work, including the establishment of Carnegie-Mellon University in 1904.

John Wesley Emerson

John Wesley Emerson was an American lawyer, American Civil War commander, Missouri Circuit Court judge, and the founder and principal investor of the Emerson Electric Company.

Eli Whitney

Eli Whitney was an American inventor best known for inventing the cotton gin. This was one of the key inventions of the Industrial Revolution and shaped the economy of the Antebellum South. Whitney's invention made upland short cotton into a profitable crop, which strengthened the economic foundation of slavery in the United States. Despite the social and economic impact of his invention, Whitney lost many profits in legal battles over patent infringement for the cotton gin.

Joseph Marie Charles Jacquard

Joseph Marie Charles Jacquard was a French weaver and merchant. He played an important role in the development of the earliest programmable loom, which in turn played an important role in the development of other programmable machines, such as an early version of digital compiler used by IBM to develop the modern day computer.

P. Banks. Beginning in 1838, he apprenticed in the shop of Ari Davis, a master mechanic in Cambridge who specialized in the manufacture and repair of chronometers and other precision instruments. It was in the employ of Davis that Howe seized upon the idea of the sewing machine.

George Westinghouse

George Westinghouse Jr. was an American entrepreneur and engineer based in Pittsburgh, Pennsylvania who invented the railway air brake and was a pioneer of the electrical industry, gaining his first patent at the age of 19. Westinghouse saw the potential in alternating current as an electricity distribution system in the early 1880s and put all his resources into developing and marketing it, a move that put his business in direct competition with the Edison direct current system. In 1911 Westinghouse received the AIEE's Edison Medal "For meritorious achievement in connection with the development of the alternating current system."

Samuel Morse

Samuel Finley Breese Morse was an American painter and inventor. After having established his reputation as a portrait painter, in his middle age Morse contributed to the invention of a single-wire telegraph system based on European telegraphs. He was a co-developer of the Morse code and helped to develop the commercial use of telegraphy.

James Bryant Conant

James Bryant Conant was an American chemist, a transformative President of Harvard University, and the first U.S. Ambassador to West Germany. Conant obtained a PhD in Chemistry from Harvard in 1916. During World War I he served in the U.S. Army, working on the development of poison gases. He became an assistant professor of chemistry at Harvard in 1919, and the Sheldon Emery Professor of Organic Chemistry in 1929. He researched the physical structures of natural products, particularly chlorophyll, and he was one of the first to explore the sometimes complex relationship between chemical equilibrium and the reaction rate of chemical processes.

Mark Twain

Samuel Langhorne Clemens, better known by his pen name Mark Twain, was an American writer, humorist, entrepreneur, publisher, and lecturer. Among his novels are The Adventures of Tom Sawyer and its sequel, the Adventures of Huckleberry Finn, the latter often called "The Great American Novel".

Elbert Hubbard

Elbert Green Hubbard was an American writer, publisher, artist, and philosopher. Raised in Hudson, Illinois, he had early success as a traveling salesman for the Larkin Soap Company. Presently Hubbard is known best as the founder of the Roycroft artisan community in East Aurora, New York, an influential exponent of the Arts and Crafts Movement. Among his many publications were the fourteen-volume work Little Journeys to the Homes of the Great and the short publication A Message to Garcia. He and his second wife, Alice Moore Hubbard, died aboard the RMS Lusitania when it was sunk by a German submarine off the coast of Ireland on May 7, 1915.

Jean Piaget

Jean Piaget was a Swiss psychologist and epistemologist known for his pioneering work in child development. Piaget's theory of cognitive development and epistemological view are together called "genetic epistemology".

Bert H. Schlain

Bert H. Schlain spent 34 years in advertising, selling, sales promotion and sales management. He was in retail and wholesale selling in many fields, sold directly for manufacturers and as a manufacturer's agent. Firms for which he established a notable sales record include Zenith Radio, General

Electric, and Universal Match Corporation, where at present he is Sales Manager of the Central States Division.

Robert Conklin

Author of How To Get People To Do Things

About the Author

David Namer's background is in real estate analysis, underwriting, and originations, with special emphasis in the development and implementation of income property, portfolio lending programs for financial institutions to maximize fee income. As well, Namer has extensive experience in sales and marketing consulting with special emphasis in the development and implementation of corporate training programs.

Namer is a consultant in sales, management, and finance. He has developed fee income programs as well as marketed financial enhancement services in conjunction with asset-based lending programs. Over the years, he has generated in excess of one hundred million dollars in fees, financing over one billion dollars in projects/assets.

Beginning in 1975, first as a captive to several Savings and Loans Associations, morphing into a service corporation for a varied conglomerate of national and international lending institutions, and finally breaking away to offers its services to the general financial and business community, Namer has provided full service, asset-based and mortgage lending services running the gamut from originations, underwriting, secondary marketing, packaging, to credit enhancement services to both the lending and the borrowing community.

As well, Namer has served in managerial and executive functions in several companies over the years. He has advanced these companies' interests in the national and international business communities, as well as broadened the base to include services rendered to business, industry, and government. Mr. Namer was responsible for the development of programs for the governments of Spain, and Tunisia, as well as provided broad based experience in marketing and sales to residential home builders and agri-business concerns in the United States and South America.

Namer was directly involved with a major life insurance company in establishing individual life and health products, establishing a nationwide agency and then staffing, recruiting, and training their sales personnel.

Namer has written a book on salesmanship and sales training entitled The People Business and has collaborated on a case study book in marketing used at the University Graduate level. Namer frequently lectured at Tulane University, University of New Orleans, University of Southeastern Louisiana, and other universities and companies on the subject of sales, marketing, and business ethics. Additionally, Namer has held direct sales positions with national and international corporations, receiving numerous sales and achievement awards for performance.

Namer was educated at Tulane University where he received a B.S. Degree. As well, he has received various degrees in Office Technology, Communications, and Business Accounting from several colleges. Mr. Namer is fluent in English, Spanish, and French, as well as conversant in other languages.

Namer is a multi-engines and instrumented rated pilot, an avid skier, tennis player, certified scuba diver, and loves to race cars and motorcycles.

www.ingramcontent.com/pod-product-compliance
Lightning Source LLC
Chambersburg PA
CBHW020538290526
45786CB00002B/939